TRACING ANCESTORS IN NORTHAMPTONSHIRE

Guidance on local, social and family history

Colin R Chapman

FIRST EDITION

Second Impression

LOCHIN PUBLISHING

Colin Chapman was born in Northampton and educated at Bedford School in the adjoining county. He has been interested in local, social and family history since the age of seven after discovering a Family Bible in his grandparents' attic in Northampton. He is a son of Don and Edna Chapman whose ancestors, stretching back for over four hundred years originate almost exclusively from Northamptonshire. Besides being an industrial chemist and nuclear engineer by profession, Colin Chapman has lectured world-wide on British social and family history since 1980; he was the first Western genealogist to be invited to speak in the former Czechoslovakia following the warming of East-West relations in 1989. He has spoken in Berlin, Heidelberg, Geneva, Paris, Vienna, Jakarta and throughout Britain and the Channel Islands on genealogically-related topics and regularly undertakes lecture tours across Canada, the United States of America, Australia and New Zealand using examples from Northamptonshire archives to illustrate his talks. He originated the three-letter Chapman County Codes for British Isles counties which formed the basis for a British Standard and now an International Standard, ISO-3166. He is the author of *The Growth of British Education & Its Records, Ecclesiastical Courts, Their Officials & Their Records, Pre-1841 Censuses & Population Listings in the British Isles, How Heavy, How Much & How Long?* (weights, money & other measures), *Using Newspapers & Periodicals* (in historical research), *Tracing Ancestors in Bedfordshire*, and *Tracing Your British Ancestors*. He is President of the Gloucestershire Family History Society, President of the Bristol & Avon Family History Society and an honorary member of the Northamptonshire Family History Society. He is a Vice-President of the international Federation of Family History Societies, a Fellow of the Society of Genealogists and a former member of its executive committee.

Cover design by Nick Ind.

Published by
LOCHIN PUBLISHING
6 Holywell Road, Dursley, GL11 5RS, England

First Edition 1994
Second Impression 1995
Copyright of the Lochin Publishing Society 1994

British Library Cataloguing in Publication Data
A catalogue record for this book is available from the British Library.
ISBN 1 873686 11 0

Northamptonshire

Northamptonshire, renowned for its spires and squires, its pillow lace and ironstone, its boots and shoes and breweries, its sons Dryden and Clare and its nephews Dodderidge and Bradlaugh, the Compton and Spencer families, the Washingtons and the Franklins, Queen Eleanor and her Crosses, and the Battles of Northampton and Naseby, lies peacefully at the heart of England, about as far from the coast as any county can be. An alphabetical list of 344 ecclesiastical parishes within Northamptonshire's ancient boundaries, with details on their administrative locations, is given in Chapter 5. A map showing the location of these is available from the County Record Office. The civil parishes and hamlets in the former administrative areas termed Hundreds are listed in Chapter 6.

The original county of Northamptonshire was subjected to changes to its civil administrative boundaries in 1888, 1965 and 1974, although these changes did not affect the ecclesiastical administrative areas. The 1888 Local Government Act created two Divisions in Northamptonshire and established a county council each for the County of the Soke (or Liberty) of Peterborough and for the remainder of Northamptonshire, apart from the County Borough of Northampton. A joint Archives Panel was formed, which included representatives from these local government areas, to ensure that the various historical records were not dispersed and lost by administrative changes. The 1888 Act also transferred parts of the parishes of Luddington, Lutton and Thurning from Huntingdonshire to Northamptonshire, and part of Winwick from Northamptonshire to Huntingdonshire. Warkworth was transferred to Oxfordshire and Little Bowden to Leicestershire.

The Soke of Peterborough joined Huntingdonshire in 1965, and Huntingdonshire became part of the joint committee, as the Archives Panel had "felt it would be a great pity if the historical and geographical associations between the Soke and the rest of Northamptonshire were severed and that the records should remain at [the Northamptonshire Record Office] if at all possible". A Chief Archivist (as distinct from a County Archivist) looked after the records. In 1974, following the 1972 Local Government Act, the Soke of Peterborough was transferred to Cambridgeshire. The same Act dissolved the neighbouring counties of Huntingdonshire and Rutland, transferring them to Cambridgeshire and Leicestershire respectively. From 1974 the Huntingdonshire representation on the Archives Panel ceased. In general the details given in the following pages refer to the county of Northampton before the boundary changes, although all addresses reflect the present situation.

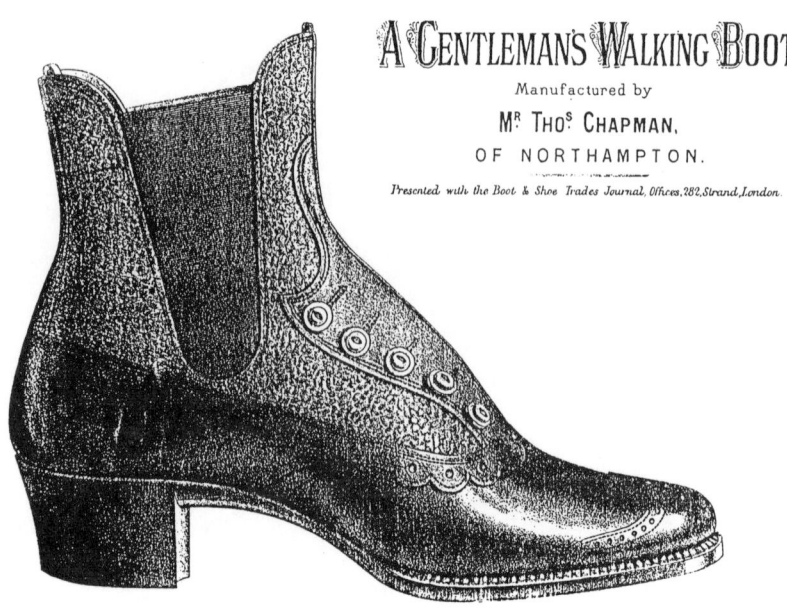

A GENTLEMAN'S WALKING BOOT

Manufactured by

MR THOS CHAPMAN,

OF NORTHAMPTON.

Presented with the Boot & Shoe Trades Journal, Offices, 282, Strand, London.

Gerald Lov' ; Penniall,Lith,9,Dyers Buildings,London E C

A GENTLEMAN'S SIDE-SPRING BOOT,
MANUFACTURED BY THE LATE MR THOMAS CHAPMAN, OF
NORTHAMPTON.

It is with feelings of the deepest regret that we have to recur to the recent decease of Mr Thomas Chapman, of St Giles's Street, Northampton. At the time of his death, the boot which forms the original of the present plate was already in the hands of our artist, and we have good reason to know that he anticipated its appearance as a supplement to the Boot and Shoe Trades Journal with no ordinary interest. Although nothing to do with our present purpose, we cannot resist the opportunity offered of expressing our sense of loss at his departure. He was one of the most companionable men we have ever had the good fortune to meet, and the regret felt at his unlooked for departure is both easily understood and accounted for.

The boot which the accompanying plate represents is, as will be seen, a fancy cut side-spring, with a mock button-piece, calf goloshed, with levant quarters, machine sewn. It is a boot well adapted to the best class of the northern trade, and when we say its design reflects credit on Northampton manufacture, we design not so much to praise the boot in question as the excellency of the work turned out by this great Midland centre of the boot and shoe industry.

From the Boot and Shoe Trades Journal, No 141, 13 March 1880.
[Thomas Chapman, the author's great grandfather died on 27 December 1879, aged 38].

Contents

Foreword

This booklet grew out of a discussion of the non user-friendly nature of the factual guides for family historians at the record office. Colin Chapman rightly thought he could do better, and this is the result.

The booklet will be especially useful if you have ancestors who lived in Northamptonshire, or if you want to use sources in Northamptonshire today to trace ancestors whose origins were elsewhere. There is guidance for beginners to genealogy and family history as well as information on sources that more advanced researchers will find useful. In spite of its slim appearance, this booklet deals with a wide range of archival sources invaluable for successful historical research. Whilst the title will attract the attention of those interested in their ancestral roots, the content offers vital assistance to local and social historians using records of past generations to recall and reconstruct communities and conditions from previous eras.

Good hunting!

RACHEL WATSON

County Archivist

Hints for Beginners to Family History

Start with your immediate family [a]. Quiz your older relatives on any family stories and ask for any documentation they may have . Certificates, newspaper cuttings, photograph albums, diaries and notebooks tucked away in cupboards and drawers may give you useful clues. Write down or record on video or audio tape the memories of your family and others in the localities frequented by your ancestors. Now work backwards from yourself....

You have a birth certificate from the civil registration system (see page 11) showing at least the name of your mother and probably your father's name as well. Assuming you are the oldest child and your parents got married around the time of your birth, you can estimate their wedding date; now obtain a marriage certificate from the same system [b] and see the exact date of the marriage, their ages and addresses, and the names and occupations of their fathers. With information on their ages you can obtain their birth certificates. You can repeat this process back to the beginning of civil registration in England and Wales on 1 July 1837, providing you with several surnames of people from whom you are directly descended.

Now look through the National Genealogical Directory [c], the Genealogical Research Directory [d], the British Isles Genealogical Register - Northamptonshire section [e], the Directories of Members' Interests for the Northamptonshire Family History Society [f] and for the Peterborough & District Family History Society [g]. These publications indicate who else is researching names and places that may coincide with your interests.

[a] See also Tracing Your British Ancestors. Colin R Chapman. Lochin Publishing. 1993. On sale at the County Record Office (CRO), Wootton Hall Park, Northampton.

[b] Original indexes at OPCS, St Catherine's House, 10 Kingsway, London, WC8 6JP;

microform copies available at Family History Centres at Northampton and Peterborough (see Chapter 7 for addresses).

Copies of certificates are available by post from OPCS, General Register Office, Postal Applications Section, Smedley Hydro, Trafalgar Road, Birkdale, Southport, Merseyside, PR8 2HH.

[c] NGD. Ed Iris Caley. published annually since 1979.

[d] GRD. Eds Keith A Johnson & Malcolm R Sainty. Published annually since 1981.

[e] Big R. Ed John Perkins. Federation of Family History Societies. 1994.

[f] Directory of Members' Interests. Northamptonshire FHS. 1986, 1989, and 1992.

[g] Directory of Members' Interests. Peterborough & District FHS. 1991 and 1994.

Next use the addresses from the civil registration certificates in conjunction with nineteenth century census returns [h] (see page 8) to discover other family members, occupations and birthplaces, possibly in Northamptonshire parishes, and even back in the eighteenth century. Consult the indexes [i] to the 1881 and 1851 census returns prepared by the Family History Societies and some local history societies. Now read the main text of this booklet.

Record, in a book or file (paper or computer), what you discover. Use a system that you, and hopefully others, can later retrieve and add to. Decide if you are going to attempt to trace all your ancestors, on both your father's and mother's sides, or to record all references to a particular surname (in which case the Guild of One Name Studies [j] may be able to help you). You should also decide whether to produce a family history (with details on your ancestors' lives and homes, even their appearances and acquaintances) or compile a family tree or pedigree chart of a fundamental genealogy.

Consider joining the Northamptonshire Family History Society [k] or the Peterborough and District Family History Society. These Societies, besides publishing quarterly journals with articles on individuals, families and parishes in Northamptonshire, hold monthly meeting in Northampton, Kettering and Peterborough, and undertake projects such as indexing census returns and parish registers and transcribing and indexing memorial inscriptions (see page 17). Go to one of their meetings where the Society members will be pleased to help you; many of them also have ancestors outside of Northamptonshire and so can advise you if you are in that position as well.

[h] Original and microform copies of returns for 1841, 1851, 1861, 1871, 1881 and 1891 are available at the Public Record Office (PRO), London;

microfilm copies of returns for the entire county for 1841 to 1891 are available at the CRO;

microfilm copies of returns for the entire county for 1861 are available in the Local Studies Collection at Northampton Central Library (NCL);

microfilm copies of returns for the north of the county for most census years are available at Peterborough Library; see Chapter 7.

[i] Indexes are available for reference at the CRO or for purchase from the Family History Societies; see ref [k].

[j] The Registrar, Box G, 14 Charterhouse Buildings, Goswell Road, London, EC1M 7BA.

[k] For addresses of current Secretaries contact the CRO or send a SAE to the Administrator, Federation of Family History Societies, Benson Room, The Institute, Margaret Street, Birmingham, B3 3BS.

Mr Richard Pickering died June ye 24 1746
And Inmitarry of his Goods and Chattels   90 . 0 . 0
Purse and Apparell — 17 . 10 . 0
Plate — 6 . 16 . 0
Furneture of the Kitchin — 2 . 0 . 0
Furneture of the Hall — 1 . 16 . 0
Furneture of the Parlo — 7 . 5 . 0
Furneture of the Parlo Chamber and Study — 3 . 16 . 0
Furneture of the Chiefe Chamber — 1 . 11 . 0
Furneture of the Butery Chamber — 1 . 0 . 0
Furneture of the Garrett — 6 . 0 . 0
Furneture of the Sollor — 2 . 0 . 0
Furneture of the Oatten Garrett — 2 . 12 . 0
Furneture of the Kilchin Chamber — 5 . 0 . 0
Furneture of the Dary — 5 . 0 . 0
Furnoture of the linen — 26 . 0 . 0
Horses Mares and Foales — 35 . 10 . 0
Cowes Hefors and Carvles — 29 . 0 . 0
Sheep and Lambs — 4 . 10 . 0
For Hogs — 144 . 0 . 0
For Foure Yard Land and halfe Crop — 14 . 10 . 0
For two Waggons and a Cart — 10 . 10 . 0
For Hovuells and Outer Woods — 0 . 5 . 0
For Five Coor Cribs — 2 . 9 . 0
Plows and Harrows — 2 . 8 . 0
Harness for Six Horses — 2 . 10 . 0
Malt Mill and two Garners — 4 . 5 . 6
For Wheat Rie and Malt — 0 . 5 . 0
Aple Mill and press —

£ 348 . 8 . 6

Tho Allowed by us
John Walton
William Chadwick

Inmitarry (Inventory) of Goods and Chattels of Richard Pickering of Bugbrook [the author's 6X great grandfather] giving also his date of death.

1. Information Already Available

Whatever aspect of history is your main interest, do not neglect the published or recorded work and research of others. Family historians can glean much from local histories while community historians would be foolish to ignore details made available by genealogists. Transcribed, translated and published material and indexes and finding aids should always be consulted before looking at original records. Family and local historians would be wise to refer to directories of pedigrees and location interests to discover if anyone else is researching the same names or parishes, with the intent to share the results of the research. There is little sense in duplicating the work of others or repeating what has already been achieved. Obviously, you will want to check other people's research; and not a few genealogies published towards the end of the nineteenth century were based on fantasy rather than fact. However, even most amazing tales contain an element of truth, and published materials, particularly if indexed, are excellent starting points.

The Northamptonshire Record Society (NRS) has been publishing annual volumes since 1924 in its Records Series, and annual volumes of *Northamptonshire Past and Present* since 1948. The Northamptonshire Family History Society (NFHS), founded in 1976, publishes a quarterly journal and regularly updates the lists of surnames and parishes in which its members are interested. The Peterborough and District Family History Society (PDFHS), founded in 1980, provides similar publications and services in the north of the county.

The proceedings and publications of the Architectural Society of the Archdeaconry of Northampton, and the Peterborough Natural History, Scientific & Archaeological Society, have many articles of interest to family and local historians, as did the *Northamptonshire History News*, first published by the Museum service from 1968 to 1987, revived as *Northamptonshire Local History News* by the Rural Community Council in 1990 and now published by Northamptonshire ACRE (Action for Communities in Rural England). Many local history groups in the county publish newsletters and magazines. The addresses of their secretaries may be obtained from the County Record Office. Even the annual publications of the Northamptonshire Natural History Society and Field Club have some items relating to historical research. National publications such as the *Genealogists' Magazine, Family Tree Magazine, Local Historian, Local Population Studies* and *Local History* are available in Northamptonshire.

The *Victoria County History* of England series has so far published only four volumes for Northamptonshire. Nevertheless, this comprehensive work provides an excellent background to the Hundreds and parishes included. There are details on manors, churches, noteworthy buildings and prominent and armigerous families.

The major repository in Northamptonshire of local and national, original and secondary material is the County Record Office (CRO); however, there are valuable collections in the Local Studies Section at the Central Library (NCL) in Northampton and at the Central Library in Peterborough and in some public libraries throughout the county (see Chapter 7 for addresses of those with important local material). The [Mormon] Family History Centres in Northampton and Peterborough, also listed in Chapter 7, have microform copies of indexes to all births, marriages and deaths for England and Wales from 1837 and of census returns for the nineteenth century; these Centres also have other material useful in genealogical and local history research, not only for Northamptonshire but for many other British and overseas areas. Unfortunately there are very few entries in the International Genealogical Index (see page 17) for Northamptonshire, although copies of parish registers are now being made available in microform at the CRO.

The museums in Daventry, Kettering, Northampton, Oundle, Peterborough and Wellingborough, and the Regimental Museums and the Police Museum in Northampton merit a visit to study their artifacts, although some of their documents are now at the CRO. There are rural life and art museums elsewhere in the county that also offer background information useful in the study of local, social and family history. The addresses of these repositories (some open only by appointment) are given in Chapter 7.

Some Northamptonshire material, especially records created by the Crown or national government, is available only at the Public Record Office (PRO) or among various manuscript collections of the British Library in London. Some classes of these records have been microfilmed and copies are available at the CRO while other items have been transcribed, translated where necessary, and published - and are also available at the CRO. There are instances, even so, when it will be necessary to look at records out of the county to trace families and ancestors in Northamptonshire.

2. Where Did Your Ancestors Live ?

Poll Books and Electoral Registers

If your ancestors were landowners or part of the lesser (or greater) gentry in Northamptonshire they (remember that only males could vote until 1918) would have been entitled to a vote. Poll books with names arranged under Hundreds, of those who voted and for whom they voted (a secret ballot is a modern concept) for the years 1695, 1702, 1705, 1730, 1748, 1806, 1831, and unusually for 1865 and 1868, are at the CRO. NCL has Poll Books of Northampton for the years 1727, 1768, 1774, 1784, 1790, 1796, 1818, 1820, 1826, 1830, 1831, 1832, 1835, 1837, 1841, 1842, 1852, 1857, 1859 and 1865. Following the 1832 Electoral Reform Bill, the entitlement to vote was extended and Electoral Registers were introduced. The CRO has registers for 1832-1970s for all Parliamentary Divisions in Northamptonshire and for Northampton Borough from 1832 to date. In boroughs throughout the country, those who were entitled to vote, mostly for borough representatives, were often termed burgesses. The Burgess Rolls of Northampton Borough for 1832-1914 are at the CRO.

Directories and Gazetteers

Towards the end of the eighteenth century court and trade directories were published throughout the country, following the successes of London directories. For over 100 years the names of only those who paid the publishers appeared in such directories; accordingly, those included are usually landowners, the gentry, the clergy and tradespeople, shopkeepers, carriers and publicans. County directories initially contained only the principal towns and listed the subscribers, often in alphabetical order. Gazetteers often included historical as well as topographical notes on the county. Some directories and gazetteers were arranged by Hundreds, later publications included smaller towns and villages, though rarely every parish, arranged in alphabetical order; large towns (eg Northampton) listed people by street and house numbers. Some directories included even street indexes; as the twentieth century progressed every householder was listed. The CRO has Trade Directories and Gazetteers of Northamptonshire between 1784 and 1940 and from 1884 to 1972 for Northampton Borough. Whellan and Kelly were the principal publishers of these works for Northamptonshire. All are on the open shelves in the Search Room at the CRO.

Census Returns

National censuses have been taken every ten years since 1801, apart from 1941. The enumerations of households were originally conducted by counties and parishes, but from 1841 the civil Registration Districts employed from 1837 were used. These Districts themselves followed the New Poor Law Union areas established in 1834. The Registration District in which each Northamptonshire parish is located is identified in Chapter 5. The early census returns required only numbers of males and females in five-year age bands to be noted; from 1841 the names, ages to the nearest five years rounded downwards, and if born in the same county (Y) or not (N), were recorded, household by household. From 1851, again by households, the names, actual age, occupation, birthplace and relationship to the head of the household for every individual were required. Only from 1841 were copies of the actual returns required in London. However, returns for Northamptonshire districts, some with names and ages of individuals for 1811, 1821 and 1831 have survived and are at the CRO.

Censuses and lists of people were taken nationally and locally long before the nineteenth century. The earliest list is the Domesday Survey of 1086. Many lists were made to raise revenue and so are taxation or subsidy rolls or lists. Poll Taxes from 1377, Hearth Taxes from 1662, Marriage Duty Taxes from 1694, Window Taxes from 1696, Land Taxes from 1752 (for Northamptonshire) and Horse Taxes, Dog Taxes, Hair Powder Taxes, to name only a few. Other lists were to identify who was fit for military service: Militia Lists and Muster Rolls. Further listings identify those who were not attending the services of the Established Church - Recusants Rolls, and Papists Lists. Other lists were for statistical purposes or curiosity; for example the Courteenhall census of 1587, the Cogenhoe censuses of 1618-28 and the Aynho census of 1740. A detailed account of dozens of pre-1841 censuses and population listings in the British Isles is given by Chapman [1].

None of the lists, made either for the decennial census returns or for other purposes, required the names to be in alphabetical order. Accordingly no indexes of names were prepared by the officials. But realising the value of the listings, Societies and individuals have transcribed and indexed (in varying quality) many of the returns. The 1881 census indexing was organised through the Federation of Family History Societies to a national standard and is undeniably the best. Some of the 1851 census indexes are of a similar quality. Some listings for parts of Northamptonshire have been published in hard copy and in microform; for example, the 1777 Militia Lists for all of Northamptonshire and those of 1762 for Nassaburgh Hundred have been published by NRS (Vols 25 and 32). The CRO has copies of the available indexes to the decennial censuses and several other population listings.

Biographical Dictionaries and Who's Whos.

If your ancestors were noteworthy in any field: writers, poets, military personnel, a mayor or Member of Parliament, a clergyman, doctor, surgeon, engineer, scientist, architect, or was a knight or Peer of the Realm, they are likely to appear in a specialist national directory or biographical dictionary, which were generally published annually or in many successive editions. In the majority of these publications the home address of the biographee is mentioned. Such national publications include *Who's Who*, first published in 1849, and *Who Was Who*, published from 1915; there was a *Cumulated Index for Who Was Who 1897-1980*. Other national directories and dictionaries include *Crockford's* (Anglican) *Clerical Directory*, from 1858, the *Catholic Directory* from 1839, the *Medical Directory* from 1845, the *Dictionary of National Biography*, the *Army List*, the *Navy List*, *Debrett's Peerage*, the *Complete Peerage* and *Burke's Commoners*. There were even some local biographies such as *Who's Who in Northamptonshire* (1935), *Who's Who in Northampton* (1961) and the fifteen-volume *Northamptonshire and Rutland Clergy* from 1500, published 1938-1945. Most of these biographical dictionaries are on the open shelves in the Search Room at the CRO. The NCL has an even wider selection of biographical dictionaries and directories.

Migration

One of the challenges in genealogy is that our ancestors appear to be constantly on the move. They do not stay at the same address, particularly in towns in the nineteenth century, although families were less likely to move than individuals searching for work or a spouse. The indexes and directories mentioned above will be helpful in locating individuals but you should consider possible migration causes and routes. In Northamptonshire the navigable rivers and particularly the Grand Junction and Grand Union Canals (from the 1790s), and the link to the River Nene opened in 1815, besides the roads and railways (from 1838) were all possible migration routes your ancestors may have used. It has been said that in the early nineteenth century Northamptonshire was transversed by more turnpiked roads than any other county in the British Isles apart from Middlesex. Coaches, long-distance waggons and short-distance carriers' carts clattered alongside pedestrian travellers. Although many people moved into towns such as Northampton, Kettering, Peterborough and Wellingborough, others did migrate from urban to rural areas for one reason or another. Others obviously moved out of the county, some even overseas, in the search for change and opportunity. The names of people leaving the British Isles were not normally listed by officialdom, although there are likely to be lists of those arriving in the former colonies such as America, Canada, Australia, New Zealand and South Africa. Genealogical and family history societies (see note k on page 3) in these countries have indexed many such passenger arrivals.

3. When Did Your Ancestors Live (& die)?

Civil Registration

The national registration of births, marriages and deaths began (as mentioned on page 2) in 1837 for England and Wales. The whole country was divided into Registration Districts, co-terminous with the Poor Law Union areas established in 1834 under the New Poor Law (see page 25). Many areas fitted within county boundaries but occasionally spilled over into an adjacent county. For example, some of the Wellingborough Union (and so the Wellingborough Registration District) covers a small part of Bedfordshire. Other Registration Districts established in 1836 for the county were Brackley, Towcester, Potterspury, Hardingstone, Northampton, Daventry, Brixworth, Kettering, Thrapston, Oundle, and Peterborough. The Districts for every parish in the county are given in Chapter 5.

An event was recorded by a local registrar who provided the informant with a certificate and sent a copy of the details via the Superintendent Registrar to the Registrar General in London, whose clerks every three months compiled national indexes of births, marriages and deaths. These indexes may be searched free of charge at St Catherine's House, London. Microform copies of the indexes are available locally (see page 2). A quarterly index entry has the name of the individual, the name of the Registration District in which the event was registered (not always when it took place) and a volume and page number of the entry in the Registrar General's files. For Northamptonshire all entries were in Volume 15 from 1837 to 1851, in Volume 3b from 1852 to March 1974, and in Volume 7 from the June quarter of 1974.

The local Registrars (see Chapter 7), to today, retain their original volumes, but having no search rooms, do not provide a public search facility. They hold only their own registers and use a totally different indexing system to that used at St Catherine's House. As a result, whilst some Registrars are able to provide copies of certificates for their Registration Districts in response to postal applications, personal callers cannot be accommodated and the St Catherine's House reference numbers are of no use at all to them.

For other parts of the British Isles such as Scotland, Ireland, the Isle of Man and the Channel Islands, civil registration commenced after 1837, although in some instances was more comprehensive than in England and Wales.

Information on civil registration systems throughout the British Isles is given in Chapman [2], available at the CRO.

Having used the civil registration birth and marriage certificates to 1837, and the nineteenth century census returns to identify birthplaces, it should now be possible to turn to a parish where an individual was born. The parish and nonconformist registers of baptisms and marriages should be used (in the same manner as civil certificates of births and marriages) to work backwards generation by generation, possibly to 1538, assuming the family remained in the same parish; many of these registers are now at the CRO, see the next four sections. If an individual cannot be found in the expected parish register, try looking in an adjacent or near-by parish; (remember the section on migration in Chapter 2). A map of Northamptonshire parishes, available from the CRO, will be very useful at this stage. In years gone by people walked much further than today to go about their daily lives. Nonconformists travelled quite long distances to attend their services and some of their ministers carried one register book from chapel to chapel. Some parishes and incumbents, often in towns, attracted couples from surprisingly long distances, perhaps offering a fashionable or discount wedding. Marriages licence records (see below) may help at this stage. Many couples often met at a local market town (see also page 20), so an old topographical map is also useful to identify pre-motorway routes. If the parish register has not survived look in the corresponding Bishop's Transcript (BT) - see below; it is worth while looking in the BTs anyway, as some events can be found there which were never entered in an original register.

Parish (Anglican) Registers

For administrative and ecclesiastical purposes the Christian Church in England and Wales was organised into the Provinces of Canterbury (in the south) and York (in the north), each headed by an archbishop; the Archbishop of Canterbury held the senior post of Primate and was originally the Pope's representative in Britain. Each province was organised into dioceses (or sees) headed by a bishop based in the cathedral city of the diocese. Dioceses were organised into archdeaconries, headed by an archdeacon who looked after several rural deaneries, divided into parishes. Each parish had a parish church in which the incumbent, a clergyman, who was a vicar, a rector or a perpetual curate, administered the Christian sacraments and conducted services in Latin. Children were baptised into the Christian faith, marriages were solemnized by the clergy and the dead were buried according to ceremonies and prayers prescribed from Rome. Some very small areas throughout the country were exempt from this administrative system.

At the Protestant Reformation, which swept across Europe in the fifteenth and sixteenth centuries, Henry VIII was declared titular head of the Anglican Church and so the Church in England became the established Church of England. The organisational structure of parishes, rural deaneries, archdeaconries, dioceses and provinces was largely retained (including the exempt areas) although six new dioceses, including Peterborough, were created in 1541. The Benedictine Abbey of Peterborough, unlike other monastic buildings in the country, was not destroyed but became Peterborough Cathedral, possibly because Henry was unwilling to destroy the burial place of his wife, Katherine of Aragon. However, during the reign of Edward VI, the forms of services were changed and the Book of Common Prayer in English was introduced. The exempt areas became known as Peculiars (see below). The rural deaneries, in which each of the Northamptonshire parishes were located until the mid-twentieth century, are given in Chapter 5; although it should be noted that these deanery names are not identical to those used today.

England has remained nominally Protestant since 1547, apart from a brief return to Catholicism during the reign of Mary (1553-1558); although during the Commonwealth (1649-1660) the civil authorities took over most of the secular duties of the Church - including the solemnization of matrimony. In 1538 the regular keeping of parish registers of baptisms, marriages and burials had begun, although not all parishes complied. Reminders to the clergy were issued in 1597 when it was also decreed that copies of the register entries should be made weekly and sent annually (on 25 March - New Year's Day until 1753) via the Archdeacon to the Bishop's Registrar in the Diocesan Registry. These contemporary copies have become known as Bishops' Transcripts (BTs).

The ecclesiastical Northamptonshire parishes listed in Chapter 5 were all in the Archdeaconry of Northampton (until 1875, when the Archdeaconry of Oakham was created, taking some parishes in the north of the county) and the Diocese of Peterborough (from its creation in 1541, apart from Thurning and Winwick All Saints, which were in Ely Diocese) and the Province of Canterbury. Rutland, until its demise in 1974, was also in the Peterborough Diocese, and in the Archdeaconry of Oakham from 1875. Prior to 1541 Northamptonshire (and Rutland) were in the Lincoln Diocese. During the nineteenth and twentieth centuries additional parishes were created to meet the requirements of increasing populations in some areas. For civil administrative purposes in 1914 the Local Government Board amalgamated the parishes of Abington, Dallington St James, Duston St James, and Kingsthorpe with the civil parish of Northampton.

There were three peculiars in Northamptonshire outside the jurisdiction of the Bishop of Peterborough: Kings Sutton in the Peculiar of Banbury, Gretton and Duddington in the Peculiar of the Prebendary of Gretton, and Nassington, Apethorpe, Wood Newton and Yarwell in the Peculiar of the Prebendary of Nassington.

Several Northamptonshire parish registers commence in 1538. The years of the first entries in each parish register are given in Chapter 5. Most Peterborough diocesan Bishop's Transcripts survive from 1706, some from 1698. About 90% of the Northamptonshire parish registers are deposited at the CRO; a complete list of those held in the county archives, with dates covered by the baptismal, marriage and burial registers, is available for purchase at the CRO. Photocopies of the surviving BTs to 1812, apart from those of Northampton, Wellingborough and Oundle, are on the open shelves in the Search Room at the CRO. The original registers and late BTs (from 1813) are available on request.

Other Ecclesiastical Records

Most people were married after the calling of banns in the parish churches where the man and woman lived. Some marriage registers had a space to record that banns had been read and on which dates; in some cases separate banns books were used. Some of these for Northamptonshire parishes are now at the CRO. It was also possible to be married after the issue of a common or ordinary licence by a bishop or an archbishop or in extreme cases after the issue of a special licence from the Faculty Office of the Archbishop of Canterbury. Associated with the issue of a common marriage licence was the Allegation or Affidavit, the Bond, the Marriage Licence Register or Act Book, the Marriage Licence itself and the subsequent entry in the marriage register of the cathedral, parish church or chapel where the marriage took place. The CRO has a card index of names of brides and bridegrooms who applied to be married by common licence in the Peterborough Diocese, in other words mostly in Northamptonshire.

The Church in years gone by was responsible for many activities now undertaken by secular authorities. The issuing of a licence to practise as a schoolmaster, a surgeon or a midwife, the adjudicating on and punishment of sexual offences, and the granting of probate (see Chapter 4) are some of the activities in which Church officials became involved, often at a sitting of an Ecclesiastical Court. The records of these Church Courts also have references to misdemeanours of the clergy and the maintenance of ecclesiastical buildings, together with the appointment of lay officials as well as the clergy within the parishes. All the extant records of the Northampton Archdeacons' Courts and the Peterborough Diocesan Courts are at the CRO.

Register Copies & Indexes

At the end of the 19th Century, William P W Phillimore an eminent genealogist, transcribed and published very many marriage registers to 1812 selected from all over the country. The only two volumes of 16 Northamptonshire parishes [3] published by Phillimore are on the open shelves at the CRO.

Rev Henry I Longden, an enthusiastic historian and antiquarian (1857-1942), undertook a great deal of biographical and genealogical research while he was rector of Heyford, particularly on the clergy and prominent families of Northamptonshire. Longden's numerous selective and incomplete notes and transcripts, of mostly marriages, of some 20 parish registers [4] and other documents are deposited at the CRO; the index to these selected transcripts is on the open shelves.

In the 1930s Percival Boyd studied and indexed hundreds of marriage registers throughout the country. Typescript copies of his indexes are deposited at the library of the Society of Genealogists. Forty-three Northamptonshire parishes [5] are included in Boyd's Miscellaneous Series.

A privately prepared and maintained index to marriages in Northamptonshire parishes is held by C Bollen Blore [6] who will respond, but only to postal enquiries.

There are many other transcripts and indexes, prepared by volunteers, held at the CRO which offer easier access to the original records.

Nonconformists, Quakers, Jews & Roman Catholics

From the Reformation in England and Wales until 1837 the only marriages recognized legally (apart from those of Quakers and Jews) were those performed by the Established (Anglican) Church. Thus everyone including nonconformists, who sought a valid wedding had the service performed in a parish church and the event recorded in a parish marriage register, normally that of the bride's residence; marriages by licence from the bishop could take place elsewhere, identified on the licence allegation. There is a card index to the marriages by licence at the CRO, arranged under surnames of potential brides and bridegrooms. Quakers and Jews were permitted to maintain their own registers. The Northamptonshire Quaker Quarterly Meeting was established in 1668 although the CRO has digests of Quaker births, marriages and burials in Northamptonshire from before this date. A considerable number of Quaker burials is also recorded in the parish register of Northampton, All Saints.

From 1837 several nonconformist meeting houses were licensed for marriages and began their own registers. Even before this some nonconformists performed their own baptisms and infant dedication ceremonies and some had their own burial grounds and conducted their own burial services; accordingly registers associated with these services were maintained. A comprehensive alphabetical summary list of Northamptonshire parish and nonconformist registers held at the CRO is available.

Jews were permitted to settle in England from 1658, having been banished in 1290, but no community appeared in Northamptonshire for many years. The first Jewish synagogue in the county was built in Overstone Road, Northampton in 1888.

Following the Reformation, the practising of Roman Catholicism was forbidden until 1791 when the building of public chapels for Roman Catholic worship was permitted; the 1829 Emancipation Act further encouraged their expansion. Accordingly there are few ancient Roman Catholic records. There are, however, Lists of Papists and Recusants Rolls which were compiled nationally in the seventeenth and eighteenth centuries. The whereabouts of this material can be ascertained at the CRO [7]. In 1676 the proportion of Catholics to the total population was lower in Northamptonshire than any other county in the province of Canterbury. Aston-le-Walls had a small Catholic community in 1688 but by 1750 Warkworth was the only one in the county, although at King's Cliffe another Mission had been established by 1778. A copy of the King's Cliffe registers from 1793 to 1855 is at the CRO. The first permanent Roman Catholic chapel in the county was opened in 1825 in Northampton.

Roman Catholic dioceses were re-established in England in 1850 and Northampton was chosen as the Cathedral Parish for the Roman Catholic Diocese of Northampton; this comprised the counties of Northamptonshire, Bedfordshire, Buckinghamshire, Cambridgeshire, Huntingdonshire, Suffolk and Norfolk. By the end of the nineteenth century there were Roman Catholic Missions in the county at Aston-le-Walls, Great Billing,

Daventry, Kettering, Oundle, Peterborough, Rushden, Weedon and Wellingborough. It should be remembered that in any case Roman Catholics were not permitted to marry other than in the Established Anglican Church until after 1836, and hence their marriages before this date will be found in parish registers.

In 1840 and again in 1858 the Registrar General requested that nonconformists and others deposit their "non-parochial" registers. These are now in the Public Record Office, London, in the RG4 to RG6 series, where they may be consulted; the CRO has microfilm copies of the non-parochial registers relating to Northamptonshire. No Roman Catholic registers for Northamptonshire were surrendered to the Registrar General, and most records are still with the Roman Catholic parish priests or in the Catholic Cathedral archives in Northampton. In recent years further nonconformist material for Northamptonshire has been deposited directly at the CRO.

International Genealogical Index (IGI)

The Genealogical Society of Utah (GSU) has been undertaking a worldwide project for many years to film and transcribe baptismal and marriage registers of all denominations. From the transcriptions, county alphabetical indexes have been published thus providing a wonderful finding aid for researchers. The indexes for English and Welsh counties were first produced in 1976 on microfiche as the Computer File Index (CFI). Published materials, such as Phillimore's transcripts and Boyd's references were also incorporated into the GSU index. When republished in 1980 it was renamed the International Genealogical Index (IGI), mentioned on page 6 above. Very few Northamptonshire parish registers have been filmed by the GSU and so the IGI coverage for the county is poor. Nevertheless, you should not neglect this extremely useful finding aid, now available on CD-ROM and microfiche. The CRO holds the 1988 microfiche edition of the IGI.

Memorial Inscriptions

Memorial inscriptions (MIs) on gravestones, tombstones, monumental brasses, church furnishings and bells at parish churches, and burial grounds and meeting houses of other denominations, often provide details on individuals not found in registers or elsewhere. Local and family historians have copied and indexed a number of the inscriptions on Northamptonshire memorials. The CRO has copies of some of these indexes. There are several indexed books on Northamptonshire monumental brasses at the CRO, NCL and libraries throughout the county.

Cemeteries

Cemeteries are grounds, other than church or chapel yards, set aside for the burial of the dead. By the early nineteenth century parish churchyards, particularly in towns, had become so full that the inadequate burial of corpses was causing not only congestion but serious health problems from the spread of diseases. As a result both private and public cemeteries were opened, the first being in Norwich in 1819. A Cemetery Clauses Act of 1847, a Public Health Act of 1848 (spurred on by dreadful outbreaks of cholera in 1846 and 1848) and a series of Burial Acts from 1850 to 1857 enabled a short-lived General Board of Health and then the Local Government Board to empower private companies and parish Burial Boards in urban and rural areas to open cemeteries. These were usually divided into consecrated and unconsecrated areas with often two or more chapels for the observance of burial services by Anglicans and Nonconformists and, later, Roman Catholics. Examples in Northamptonshire are the Northampton General Cemetery Company which was incorporated in 1846 and completed the Billing Road Cemetery in 1847; Oundle Cemetery was opened in 1859 and Kettering Cemetery in 1861. Cemetery records normally include the location of graves, names of grave purchasers and dates of purchase, besides the names of the persons buried, the date of burial and sometimes the date of death as well. For cemeteries in Northamptonshire these records are now with the local councils which have assumed responsibility for the cemeteries from the Burial Boards. The CRO has a list of cemeteries in the county.

4. How Did Your Ancestors Live ?

Trades, Occupations and Professions

A few enthusiastic historians and organisations are compiling national and local indexes of individuals involved in particular trades and occupations. The Northampton Central Museum has a national index of thousands of firms and individual shoemakers (1700 to date). An index of woadpeople (1650-1851), mostly from Northamptonshire is held by Mrs V Billington in Bath [8]. An index of canal and river boatmen and allied trades working on inland waterways is held by Mr J Roberts of Sutton Coldfield [9]. The CRO has a limited Personal Names Index and an Occupations Index on cards which lead you to documents held in the County Archives and in Northampton Central Library. Trades Directories and Biographical Dictionaries (see Chapter 2) provide details of the more affluent traders and professionals in the county.

Newspapers

Increasingly in the nineteenth century, newspapers reported a variety of social events as well as other news items. The *Northampton Mercury*, established in 1720, is one of the oldest local newspapers and has the longest continuous run of any British provincial newspaper. Notices of births, marriages and deaths, obituaries and reports on funerals, on court cases and local events became very popular from the end of the 1800s. The Mercury covered news from neighbouring counties for over 150 years even after their own local papers were founded. Some of the county-related papers were the *Huntingdon, Bedford and Peterborough Weekly Gazette*, founded in 1813, the *Northampton Herald* in 1831, the *Peterborough Advertiser* in 1854, the *Northampton Daily Chronicle* in 1880, the *Rutland, Oundle and Stamford Post* in 1885, and the *Northampton Independent* in 1905. The CRO has a collection of some of these and many other local newspapers and of the *Illustrated London News*.

NCL has a comprehensive collection of local newspapers in hard copy and on microfilm. Peterborough Library and St Ives Library have some of the Peterborough papers. A comprehensive list of Northamptonshire newspapers appeared in the 5th issue of *Northamptonshire History News*, 1972. The Northampton Central Museum has a complete run of the *Boot and Shoe Trades Journal* from 1878 to 1921, and of the *Shoe and Leather Record* from

1910 to 1943 and its successor to the present, containing many references to Northamptonshire individuals and firms involved in the boot and shoe trades.

Markets and Fairs

If your ancestors were involved in any form of trading - buying or selling, agricultural products or livestock - this would have been undertaken at one or more of the weekly or biweekly markets held all over the country. Much larger trading fairs were also held in some towns several times a year and at which entertainment was often provided; some fairs were for hiring seasonal or more permanent workers, whereas towards the end of the nineteenth century others were entirely for pleasure. Some markets and fairs were established by Royal Charters and are of very ancient origin. Forty-nine Northamptonshire, mostly mediaeval, markets and fairs were identified by Peter Goodfellow in 1987/8 [10]. Many, but certainly not all, were held on the patronal festival day of the dedication of the parish church. As many couples, possibly your ancestors, first met at a market or fair, an appreciation of Northamptonshire market towns and the days on which the markets and fairs flourished is helpful in tracing their movements. The market towns can be located on old maps, eg, Saxton (1576), Speed (1601) and Bowen (1760); but a useful gazetteer of the county's markets and fairs from 1086 to 1700 was included by Goodfellow in his article. The following list applied in 1874 but the popularity of markets and fairs rose and fell as the nineteenth century progressed; several traditional market days and dates of annual fairs were changed. Even in 1830 places such as Aynho, Fawsley, Higham Ferrers and Rockingham were described as "former Market Towns". By the First World War many markets and fairs had ceased altogether; by 1930 the nature of the weekly market had changed and annual fairs were held only in Brackley, Daventry, Fotheringhay, Kettering, Northampton, Oundle, Peterborough, Rockingham, Rothwell, Thrapston, Great Weldon and Wellingborough.

Boughton: Annual cattle, horse and pleasure fair on 24-26 June.

Brackley: Market day Wednesday.
Annual fairs on Wednesday after 25 February, 19 April, Wednesday after 22 June, Wednesday after Old Michaelmas Day (11 October), pleasure fair on 11 December.

Brigstock: Annual fairs on 25 April, 4 September, for cattle and pleasure on 22 November.

Brixworth: Annual pleasure fair on 5 June.

Daventry: Market day Wednesday.

Annual fairs on second Tuesdays in February and March, Easter Tuesday, 9 May, first Monday and 6-7 June (St Augustine's), second Tuesday in July, 3 August and last Monday in August, second Tuesday in September, for cheese on 2 October, 3, 27 November and second Tuesday in November, for cattle on second Tuesday in December.

[Annual hiring fairs on the two next Wednesdays after Michaelmas Day were discontinued by 1874].

Flore: Annual feast on first Sunday in November (instituted after 1874).

Fotheringhay: Annual horse, cattle and pleasure fairs on third Monday after 5 July.

Haddon, West: Annual cattle fairs on 2 May and hiring fairs on last Friday in September.

Higham Ferrers: Former market day Saturday but reinstated about 1900 on a Monday.

Annual fairs on Tuesday before 5 February, 6 March, Thursday before Old May Day (12 May), 28 June, Thursday before 5 August, 11 October, for cattle on 6 December.

Kettering: Market day Friday.

Annual fairs on Thursday before Easter, Friday before Whit Sunday, Thursday before 11 October, for sheep and cattle on Thursday before St Thomas Day (21 December).

Annual week-long feast from Sunday after St Peter's Day (29 June).

King's Cliffe: Annual cattle and cheese fairs on Tuesday before 29 October.

Long Buckby: Former market day Tuesday (discontinued long before 1830). Annual fairs on 1 May and for cattle on 11 October.

Moreton Pinkney: Cattle market every other Monday instituted about 1900.

Northampton: Market days Wednesday (formerly Monday), Friday and for cattle on Saturday.

Annual fairs on second Tuesday in January, 20 February, third Monday in March, 5 April, 4 May, 19 June, 5 and 26 August, for cheese on 19 September, first Thursday in November, 28 November, for cattle on Friday before Great Smithfield Market. An annual wool fair is held in July.

Annual hiring fairs on first and second Tuesdays after 29 September.

Oundle: Market day Thursday.
Annual fairs on 25 February and for horses on six preceding days, Whit Monday and for stock and pedlary on 12 October.

Peterborough: Market day Saturday.
Annual fairs (St Peter's) on 10 July, for cattle, horses and wool on 11 July, 2 October and a general purpose (Bridge) fair on 3 October.

Rockingham: Annual cattle fair on 25 September.

Rothwell: Annual three-day stock and general produce fair from Trinity Monday.

Thrapston: Market day Tuesday for corn, seed and hogs.
Annual fairs on first Tuesday in May, for sheep, cattle and pleasure on Tuesday after 11 October.
Former annual (St James') hiring fair for harvestmen on 5 August.

Towcester: Market day Tuesday.
Annual fairs on Shrove Tuesday, 12 May, for cattle on 29 October.

Weldon, Great: Former market day Wednesday.
Annual fairs on first Thursdays in February, May, August and November.

Wellingborough: Market day Wednesday.
Annual fairs for cattle on Wednesday in Easter week, for pleasure in Wednesday in Whitsun week, for sheep and cattle on 29 October.

Yardley Hastings: Annual fair on Whit Tuesday.

Educational Establishments

Education in the British Isles was promoted by the Church from the seventh century when schools (still existing today) were established in Canterbury, Rochester and York. The universities of Oxford and Cambridge were founded in the twelfth century. Prior to the Reformation, monasteries and nunneries respectively offered education for boys and girls. In very many villages the parish priest held a school, usually in the church, often over the south porch or in the tower. After the Reformation and Civil War, and religious toleration gained favour, dissenters established their own schools and academies for their adherents and their children. From the fifteenth century schools were founded and endowed by wealthy merchants to teach the skills of reading, writing and arithmetic to potential recruits (irrespective of denominational loyalty) to their expanding businesses as international trade developed alongside world exploration. Many such schools evolved into grammar and public schools whose records, in many cases, stretch from their foundation to the present.

Charity schools were established from the end of the seventeenth century which enabled even the poorest children to be provided not only with education but clothing, food and boarding. These "hospital schools", funded by bodies like SPCK, had such distinctive clothing that they were termed Blue Coat, Green, Yellow or Red Coat Schools, as appropriate. Military schools offered education for children of soldiers and sailors and even civilians who worked at related establishments such as dockyards. From the early nineteenth century National Schools (using the ideas of Bell, an Anglican clergyman) and British Schools (using similar ideas of Lancaster, a Quaker) spread throughout the country. Village Schools, Dame Schools and private institutions, Reformatory Schools for boys and girls and adult schools were opened as the nineteenth century progressed. A 1830 list of many schools in Northamptonshire is available at the CRO. By the First World War there was a school in every or a nearby parish.

Many schools kept admissions registers and log books, management, governors or board minutes, awards and punishment books with records of teachers and pupils. In some cases the funding body has the documentation today, in other cases the records are still at the school. The CRO has some records of Northamptonshire schools in all of the above categories. Some of the older schools founded in the county are at Brackley (1447), Higham Ferrers (1420), Northampton (1551), Oundle (1556), King's School Peterborough (1540) and Wellingborough (1595).

The names of students at Oxford and Cambridge Universities have been recorded in Alumni Oxoniensis and Alumni Cantabrigiensis, copies of which are on the open shelves in the Search Room at the CRO. Considerably more detail on the growth of British education, and its records of particular use to family historians, is available [11] from the CRO.

Probate

You may be able to discover a great deal on how your ancestors lived, their occupations, the crops they grew, the sizes of their homes, descriptions of their worldly possessions and an indication of their wealth, social status and friends from probate material - their wills, inventories, or Letters of Administration (Admons), if they died intestate.

The Established Church was responsible for probate - proving wills and granting Admons until 1858. The Ecclesiastical Court in which probate was granted depended on where the deceased lived or died and owned property, and the value of the estate. The CRO has details [12] on the range of ecclesiastical courts and of procedures followed in them. Testators in Northamptonshire are likely to have had probate granted on their behalf in the Court of the Archdeacon of Northampton, or in the Consistory Court of the Bishop of Lincoln (until 1541) or of the Bishop of Peterborough (after 1541), or possibly in the Prerogative Court of the Archbishop of Canterbury (PCC); this was because the county is in the Archdeaconry of Northampton, was in the Diocese of Lincoln until 1541 (and thereafter in the Diocese of Peterborough) and is in the Province of Canterbury. The original Northamptonshire probate records for the archdeaconry and the Peterborough diocesan courts to 1858 are at the CRO. The Lincoln Diocesan material relating to Northamptonshire (before 1541) is in the Lincolnshire Record Office.

P I King's detailed guide to the wills held at the CRO is in the Search Room, as are card indexes to the 1726-1858 Northampton Archdeaconry Court wills and the 1719-1858 Peterborough Consistory Court wills. There are also bound calendars (alphabetical indexes under the initial letter only) of earlier probate material. The PCC probate material is held at the PRO, London. The British Record Society (BRS) has published and indexed names of the testators of Wills 1510-1652 from the Northampton Archdeaconry Court records [13], and of Admons 1677-1710 [14] and 1711-1800 [15]. Indexes to Wills and Admons from the PCC from 1383 have also been published by the BRS [16], which has additionally published [17] indexes to the Wills and Admons from the Peculiar Courts of Gretton (1657-1832) and Nassington (1702-1744). An index to the probate of the Peculiar of Banbury (1547-1856) has been published by the Oxfordshire Record Society [18]. The volumes cited above are available on the open shelves in the Search Room at the CRO and in most large public reference libraries.

In 1858 the Ecclesiastical Probate Courts were closed and Civil Probate Courts and registries were opened; copies of the granted probate were sent to the Principal Probate Registry, Family Division, now at Somerset House, London [19], indexed alphabetically in annual volumes for the whole of England and Wales. These may be consulted free of charge in London and copies of the probate documents purchased for a modest fee. Northamptonshire came under the Northampton and the Peterborough (civil) Probate Registries. The CRO has a card index to the Northampton (civil) Probate Wills 1858-1930 and to the Peterborough (civil) Probate Registry

Wills 1858-1941. The original documentation relating to this probate material is at the Birmingham District Probate Registry [20].

The Old and New Poor Laws

Social security has been available in one form or another in England and Wales for over a thousand years. Originally provided by the Monarch, and also with shelter, food and clothing being available in mediaeval monasteries and abbeys, it became administered locally but somewhat loosely from the fifteenth century. A series of Poor Laws in the sixteenth and seventeenth centuries tightened up who was entitled to relief and under what conditions. The dole was distributed from parochially collected funds by Overseers of the Poor elected annually at a meeting of the Parish Vestry. Living or working in a parish for a year were generally suitable qualifications for eligibility for relief; but the many disputes regarding entitlement and cases of removing paupers to their birthplaces (or places of legal settlement), were brought before the local magistrates at the Quarter Sessions. Dubious cases were examined, illegally settled persons ordered to be removed and fathers of illegitimate children were ordered to pay towards their upkeep. An unmarried mother was required to name the father of her bastard child and a warrant was issued for his arrest if his ready support was not forthcoming. Illegitimate children were taught skills through parochially-organised apprenticeships in an attempt to reduce the potential drain on parish funds brought about by unskilled, unemployable residents entitled to relief.

Workhouses, providing in-door relief, began to be built for the infirm poor in the eighteenth century, but the whole social security system became so thoroughly corrupt that a New Poor Law was introduced in 1834. The administration was vested in Guardians of the Poor responsible for Poor Law Union areas - each named after the location of its workhouse. The Unions to which each Northamptonshire parish was assigned are given in Chapter 5. Lying-in rooms in the workhouses later developed into hospitals.

Some of the administration of the Old Poor Laws thus fell on the shoulders of county magistrates and was dealt with at Quarter Sessions, whilst parish overseers, churchwardens and constables also became involved in their regular implementation. The New Poor Laws additionally involved the Guardians. The documentation associated with the Old and New Poor Laws is, therefore, dispersed in several different files in archives across the country. The Northamptonshire CRO, in parish and quarter sessions and other records in connection with the Old Poor Laws, has many settlement certificates, examination papers, removal orders, bastardy bonds, warrants for arrests of erring fathers, apprenticeship indentures, overseers' accounts and constables' accounts and notebooks. From 1834 there are Poor Law Guardians' minutes, numerous ledgers, vouchers, receipt and account books, outdoor relief books, admission and dicharge books, birth and death registers, day books and journals, visitors' books, medical reports and hospital records, and mounds of correspondence relating to the social security in Northamptonshire until 1929, when central government took over the entire system. The CRO has a personal names index to the Settlement Papers in the Northamptonshire parish records list. NCL has some minutes from 1835-36 and 1839-44 for meetings of the Northampton Poor Law Union Guardians, and some later financial accounts.

In addition to the Poor Law records held at the CRO and NCL, there are vast amounts of documentation at the PRO in the MH series. In MH12 alone there are over 16,000 volumes of correspondence between the local Guardians and the Poor Law Commission to 1847 and the Poor Law Board after that. The Northamptonshire material from 1834 to 1900 is arranged by Unions in MH12/8671-8926 and 16727-16741; later correspondence is in MH68 if it survived destruction during the Second World War. There is some interesting correspondence between 1837 and 1876 in MH19/22 regarding emigration of paupers. MH9 and MH19 contain information on various officers appointed in each Union from 1837 to 1921, while MH27 deals with schooling for the poor from 1848 to 1910. Do not forget that some Northamptonshire parishes on the county boundary fell into Unions associated with other counties and so their New Poor Law records are likely to be found there.

Parish and Borough Records

The parish church registers of baptism, marriage and burial have been described in Chapter 3; the parish as an administrative unit for collecting and distributing poor law relief by overseers appointed at a Vestry Meeting was mentioned in the previous section. The parish, as both an ecclesiastical and a secular entity, and the borough in urban areas, influenced almost every aspect of the lives of your ancestors, creating many records now in the CRO that can be used today to discover more about them. The decisions taken at meetings of the Vestry (originally all the parishioners and later selected or elected persons to represent them) were recorded in Vestry Minutes. Vestries developed into Parish Councils in rural areas and into Borough Councils, and later District Councils, in urban areas. Today Parochial Church Councils look after local ecclesiastical matters but years ago the Vestry approved the appointment of Churchwardens and Parish Clerks and looked after Glebe Terriers - records of Church property.

Besides the secular office of Overseer of the Poor, the Vestry appointed an Overseer of the Highway or Waywarden, a Hedgewarden, a Constable and his assistant the Pindar or Keeper of the Pound, a host of other parish appointments, and dealt with the Enclosure and Tithe Commutation Acts of the early nineteenth century. Many parish officials recorded their activities and maintained accounts which were submitted to the Vestry for approval. The Constable, for example, was responsible for listing Militiamen, keeping law and order and taking those who defaulted to magistrates at petty or quarter sessions (see next section), recording these events in notebooks. Most parishes were endowed with a modest charity, some associated with schooling, set up by a local benefactor, for which accounts were kept. The parish filing system for all these documents, terriers, minutes, accounts and notebooks was a wooden chest in the church. Most of this material from the Parish Chests is now at the CRO although some, such as the Kettering Vestry Minutes (1797-1853) and the Peterborough Churchwardens' Accounts (1467-1573) have been transcribed, indexed and published by NRS in annual Volumes 6 (1933) and 9 (1939), and so are available in libraries throughout the county.

An excellent survey of documents generated by a typical borough administration can be found in J Charles Cox's 'Records of the Borough of Northampton 1550-1835' Vol 2, published in 1898 and on the open shelves in the search room at the CRO and at NCL. Cox describes items such as civic jurisdiction, town properties, public health, trades, freemen, apprentices, charities, churches, military matters and topography; he also included lists of names from the thirteenth to the nineteenth centuries of mayors, bailiffs, chamberlains, town clerks, stewards, serjeants-at-mace, town criers and masters of the Grammar School. The CRO has many Northamptonshire borough archives, such as these, and can advise on the whereabouts of others in the county.

Manorial and Land Records

In addition to the Church and central and local government being interested in the welfare of your ancestors and the services your ancestors could return to these systems, the lords of the manors operated in a third distinct and ancient administrative system associated with land tenure, particularly in rural areas. In towns it was possible to buy freedom from the land tenure system. Even before the Norman invasion of 1066 most land belonged to the king who let portions of it to his vassals under certain conditions, normally providing military or agricultural services. William I reinforced this system but enabled the greater and lesser barons, the lords, to let portions of their lands, their manors, to tenants under similar conditions of servitude although the lords still rendered homage to the king. Copyhold tenure, and gradually freehold, and finally leasehold tenure grew from the manorial system.

A series of Manorial Courts was set up to administer the procedures, collect rents and admonish those who failed to pay or broke certain terms of the tenures. The records of the Courts Baron, Leet and Customary, in Latin until 1733, are useful for family historians because copyhold tenure enabled land to be passed from generation to generation with the approval of the manorial court - and at certain court sittings the names of all the tenants are listed. Because manorial records and rolls were regarded as the lord's or his steward's personal documents, many have not been deposited in official archives, and those that are deposited are in a variety of places. However, the Manorial Documents Register of the Historical Manuscripts Commission [21] has a complete list of the locations of all known manorial documents. The CRO has some manorial records for Northamptonshire manors. Some manorial records, eg, for Wellingborough Manor 1258-1323, have been transcribed, translated, indexed and published by the Northamptonshire Record Society [22].

Associated with manorial records from the thirteenth to the seventeenth centuries are Inquisitiones Post Mortem (Questions After Death, asked by the Crown when a landowner died if the sovereign had an interest in the land) and Extenta Manerii (descriptions of the manors of the deceased). Although in Latin and kept at the PRO, these records can supply useful genealogical data as a landowner's heir and age are stated.

From time to time, individuals and bodies (both ecclesiastical and secular authorities) who acquired the ownership of parcels of land chose to let or lease that land or transfer it by sale or otherwise to other individuals or bodies. Deeds and maps with names of owners and occupiers, landlords and tenants, were drawn up. Many of these documents regarding land in Northamptonshire are now at the CRO. Enclosure Awards and Tithe Maps and Schedules, giving names of individuals, perhaps your ancestors, are also at the CRO.

Quarter Sessions and Assizes

Magistrates, originally as Keepers of the Peace and then Justices of the Peace, have been appointed in every shire and county for hundreds of years. They normally met in sessions every three months. The records maintained by Clerks of Peace of these Quarter Sessions are full of names, probably of your ancestors. The justices and clerks dealt with law and order, and so maintained rolls and files, record and order books, presentments, depositions of witnesses and recognizances and lists of jurors and also kept lists of freeholders. However, they also supervised the administration of the Poor Laws and issued numerous licences for activities such as killing or keeping game, operating alehouses and nonconformist chapels and printing presses in return for taxes or duties paid. If anyone, perhaps also your ancestors, failed to comply with the regulations to serve or pay or obtain a licence, the magistrates passed sentence.

Do not forget that some offences, particularly of a moral nature, were dealt with by Church officials at sittings of Ecclesiastical Courts (see page 14). Certain elements of law and order were settled by the Manorial Courts (see above). Forest Courts (Swanimotes) dealt with various aspects of life in the parishes of Northamptonshire's Royal Forests, Rockingham, Whittlewood (Whittlebury) and Salcey.

Serious offences were referred to judges on circuit at Assizes which were generally held twice a year. Northamptonshire was in the Midland Circuit, apart from the period 1864 to 1876 when it was in the Norfolk Circuit. The names of individuals held in gaol, prior to appearing at Quarter Sessions or Assizes, or as a result of a sentence held in goal prior to transportation or committed to the House of Correction are on goal lists, many of which have survived. Coroners, elected by freeholders until 1888 and appointed by county councils thereafter, were responsible for investigating sudden, unnatural or suspicious deaths and deaths in prisons.

Assize records such as Minute Books, Indictments and Depositions, and County Prisons Registers, Calendars of Prisoners, Criminal Registers and Petitions from Criminals and their Families, are at the PRO [23], although some material for the Midland Circuit is missing. Included among the many records in the CRO for Quarter Sessions held in Northamptonshire are Jury Lists (1823-1923), Freeholders Lists (1699-1926), Alehouse Keepers' Recognizances (1692 and 1737-1828), Quarter Sessions Rolls and Files (1630 and 1657-1972), Minute Books (1668-1965), Record and Order Books (1685-1707 and 1738-1962), Presentments (1693-1980) and Recognizances (1672-1846). There is a card index to the Record Book 1730-1754 in the Search Room.

The CRO holds some Quarter Sessions records specifically for Northampton Borough, ie, Rolls and Files (1745-1902) with Depositions from 1880. There are also records of Quarter Sessions held in Peterborough: Rolls and Files (1623-1632, 1699-1710, 1872-1917 and 1923-1965), and Record and Order Books (1756-1787 and 1795-1965). The Northamptonshire Quarter Sessions records for 1630, 1657 and 1657-58 were transcribed and indexed by Joan Wake and published by NRS in 1924 as Volume 1 in their series, available on the open shelves in the Search Room at the CRO. Detail on the Royal Forests of the county, including the Swanimotes and the whereabouts of their records, some at the CRO, some at the PRO, was published by the NRS in 1968 (in Vol 23); this work, containing an excellent bibliography is on the open shelves at the CRO and is available at NCL and libraries throughout the county. Coroners records for Northamptonshire until the fifteenth century are in the PRO; material from the nineteenth century is in the CRO, although the records are closed for 75 years. However, reports of inquests can often be found, vividly described in many cases, in local newspapers.

Military Ancestors

The regular (Standing) army has its pure origins in 1661 when the unconstitutional New Model of Oliver Cromwell was being disbanded by Charles II and the Restoration Parliament. There had always been (since 1181 at least) a territorial force; the Assize of Arms in that year required all freemen over the age of fifteen to keep weapons in their homes, initially to "abate the power of felons" and keep the peace but in reality to act as a Militia (although that term was not used until 1641) for the defence of the country. Apart from 1916-19 and 1939-60, when Britain used conscription for its military forces, the regular army has comprised volunteers who had chosen a military life-time career for one reason or another. A naval fleet, from which the Royal Navy developed, was constitutionally recognized well over 200 years before the army, perhaps because it posed a limited threat in a possible civil war. The Marines, established in 1690, became the Royal Marines in 1802. The Royal Air Force grew out of the Royal Flying Corps in 1918.

Colonel James Cholmondeley's Regiment of Foot was raised in 1740, renamed the 48th Foot in 1751 and again renamed in 1782 as the 48th (Northamptonshire) Foot. From 1881 this became the 1st Battalion of the Northamptonshire Regiment, the 2nd Battalion being the former 58th (Rutlandshire) Regiment of Foot. In 1960 the Northamptonshire Regiment was amalgamated with the Royal Lincolnshire Regiment and became the 2nd East Anglian Regiment (Duchess of Gloucester's Own Royal Lincolnshire and Northamptonshire). This was redesignated in 1964 and again in 1968 when it became the 2nd Battalion, The Royal Anglian Regiment. The principal battles and campaigns in which the Northamptonshire Regiment and its predecessors the 48th and 58th Regiments of Foot, participated are given in Chapter 7; those at which Honours on the Colours were received are identified.

In tracing the service career of a military ancestor you should refer to the records of the Army, Royal Navy, Royal Marines or Royal Air Force which are at the PRO in London (Kew). Further details on military records are given in Tracing Your British Ancestors [24] available from the CRO. A few Northamptonshire Regimental archives are held at the CRO and the Regimental Museum is well worth a visit. All these addresses are in Chapter 7.

For Northamptonshire Militiamen of the sixteenth and seventeenth centuries, volumes 3, 7 and 27 of the NRS annual series provide excellent information, while volumes 25 and 32 have indexed listings of some eighteenth century Militiamen in the county. There are Muster Rolls and Books, Ballot Lists and Posse Comitatus Lists at the CRO and at the PRO. The CRO can advise on what is available.

Heraldry

If you believe that one of your ancestors was armigerous (was granted an armorial achievement - a coat of arms - by the College of Arms), that fact will have been recorded by one of the heralds. You should appreciate that there is no such thing as a Family Coat of Arms. An individual was given a coat of arms by a herald on behalf of the monarch for services rendered to the Crown. Under specific circumstances the children of an armiger could also display the arms of their father, indicated with some mark of difference; this, and their pedigree, had to be registered with the heralds at the College. In the sixteenth and seventeenth centuries the heralds travelled the country on their visitations, to check who was displaying which arms and to record their pedigrees from the original armiger. The pedigrees recorded were not always complete; embarrassing or inconsequential family members were conveniently forgotten and occasionally some "ancestors" were found to add prestige to a family. As a consequence Visitation Pedigrees should be verified from other sources wherever possible. The heralds visited Northamptonshire in 1564, 1617 and 1618 and again in 1681. Copies of the Heralds' Visitations for Northamptonshire were published in 1887 and 1935 and are available at the CRO. Sir Christopher Hatton's Book of Seals was published by NRS in 1950.

When armigers died, their coats of arms were paraded on hatchments at their funerals. After a ceremony a funeral hatchment was sometimes hung in the parish church; in many Northamptonshire churches such hatchments are still there to this day. Two very nice manuscript volumes on Northamptonshire hatchments by K R J Kitchin, based on a 1910 book by C A Markham, are held at the CRO.

During the late eighteenth and throughout the nineteenth and twentieth centuries, numerous books have been published on coats of arms that were awarded to individuals ranging from the lower ranks of the gentry to royal dukes. Copies of many of these publications are at the CRO and at NCL and other libraries throughout the county.

Arms of some Bishops of Peterborough 1541-1864

5. Northamptonshire Parishes

Northamptonshire ecclesiastical parishes are listed in this chapter. They are arranged in alphabetical order, with the date of the first entry in a register, the original Rural Deanery (Dn) and portion 1, 2, or 3 where relevant, or a Peculiar (Pec), the Hundred (Hd) or Borough (Bor), and the Poor Law Union (Un), and thus the Registration District, in which each parish originally appeared.

In many cases there are gaps in the register entries. Where an earlier register has recently been lost or severely damaged, this is indicated by †. Other footnotes are explained at the end of the list. A full list of the registers held at the CRO of baptisms, marriages and burials is available from the county archives.

Abington 1637; Dn Haddon 2; Hd Spelhoe; Un Northampton. [L]

Abthorpe 1583; Dn Brackley 2; Hd Towcester; Un Towcester. [L]

Addington, Great 1693; Dn Higham Ferrers 1; Hd Huxloe; Un Thrapston.

Addington, Little 1588; Dn Higham Ferrers 1; Hd Huxloe; Un Thrapston.

Adstone 1678; Dn Brackley 1; Hd Greens Norton; Un Towcester.

Alderton 1597; Dn Preston 2; Hd Cleley; Un Potterspury.

Aldwinckle All Saints 1653; Dn Higham Ferrers 2; Hd Huxloe; Un Thrapston.

Aldwinckle St Peter 1653; Dn Higham Ferrers 2; Hd Huxloe; Un Thrapston.

Althorpe (ex-par)(used Gt Brington regs); Hd Nobottle Grove; Un Brixworth.

Apethorpe 1676; Pec; Hd Willybrook; Un Oundle.

Arthingworth 1650; Dn Rothwell 2; Hd Rothwell; Un Mkt Harborough.

Ashby St Ledgers 1554; Dn Daventry; Hd Fawsley; Un Daventry.

Ashley 1588; Dn Weldon 1; Hd Corby; Un Mkt Harborough.

Ashton 1682; Dn Preston 2; Hd Cleley; Un Potterspury.

Aston le Walls 1538; Dn Brackley 1; Hd Chipping Warden; Un Banbury.

Aynho 1562; Dn Brackley 3; Hd Kings Sutton; Un Brackley.

Badby 1559; Dn Daventry; Hd Fawsley; Un Daventry.

Bainton 1713; Dn Peterborough 2; Hd Nassaburgh; Un Stamford.

Barby 1538; Dn ; Hd Fawsley; Un Rugby.

Barford (ex-par); Hd Rothwell; Un Kettering.

Barnack 1696; Dn Peterborough 2; Hd Nassaburgh; Un Stamford. [B]

Barnwell All Saints 1558; Dn Oundle 1; Hd Huxloe; Un Oundle.

Barnwell St Andrew (used Barnwell All SS regs); Dn Oundle 1; Hd Polebrook; Un Oundle.

Barton Seagrave 1609; Dn Weldon 2; Hd Huxloe; Un Kettering.

Beanfield Lawns (ex-par)(used Cottingham regs); Hd Corby; Un Kettering.

Benefield 1570; Dn Oundle 1; Hd Polebrook; Un Oundle.

Billing, Great 1662; Dn Haddon 2; Hd Spelhoe; Un Northampton.

Billing, Little 1632; Dn Haddon 2; Hd Spelhoe; Un Northampton.

Blakesley 1538; Dn Brackley 2; Hd Greens Norton; Un Towcester.

Blatherwycke 1621; Dn Oundle 2; Hd Corby; Un Oundle.

Blisworth 1551; Dn Preston 2; Hd Wymersley; Un Towcester.

Boddington 1558; Dn Brackley 1; Hd Chipping Warden; Un Banbury.

Borough Fen (ex-par)(used Newborough regs); Hd Nassaburgh; Un Peterborough.

Boughton 1549; Dn Haddon 2; Hd Spelhoe; Un Brixworth.

Bowden, Little 1653; Dn Rothwell; Hd Rothwell; Un Mkt Harborough. [B] [x]

Bozeat 1729; Dn Higham Ferrers 1; Hd Higham Ferrers; Un Wellingborough.

Brackley 1560; Dn Brackley 3; Hd Kings Sutton; Un Brackley. [B]

Bradden 1559; Dn Brackley 2; Hd Greens Norton; Un Towcester. [L]

Brafield-on-the-Green 1653; Dn Preston 1; Hd Wymersley; Un Hardingstone.

Brampton Ash 1580; Dn Weldon 1; Hd Corby; Un Mkt Harborough.

Braunston 1538; Dn Daventry; Hd Fawsley; Un Daventry.

Braybrooke 1653; Dn Rothwell 2; Hd Rothwell; Un Mkt Harborough.

Brigstock 1641; Dn Higham Ferrers 2; Hd Corby; Un Thrapston.

Brington 1558; Dn Haddon 2; Hd Nobottle Grove; Un Brixworth.

Brixworth 1546; Dn Rothwell 3; Hd Orlingbury; Un Brixworth.

Brockhall 1561; Dn Weedon; Hd Nobottle Grove; Un Daventry. [L]

Broughton 1560; Dn Rothwell 1; Hd Orlingbury; Un Brixworth. [B]

Bugbrooke 1556; Dn Weedon; Hd Nobottle Grove; Un Northampton. [L]

Bulwick 1563; Dn Oundle 2; Hd Corby; Un Oundle.

Burton Latimer 1538; Dn Weldon 2; Hd Huxloe; Un Kettering.

Byfield 1636; Dn Brackley 1; Hd Chipping Warden; Un Daventry.

Canons Ashby 1696; Dn Brackley 1; Hd Greens Norton; Un Daventry. [L]

Carlton, East 1625; Dn Weldon; Hd Corby; Un Kettering.

Castle Ashby 1564; Dn Preston 1; Hd Wymersley; Un Hardingstone.

Castor 1538; Dn Peterborough 1; Hd Nassaburgh; Un Peterborough. [B] [P]

Catesby 1705; Dn Daventry; Hd Fawsley; Un Daventry.

Chacombe 1566; Dn Brackley 3; Hd Kings Sutton; Un Banbury.

Chapel Brampton (civil par)(used Church Brampton regs); Hd Nob'tle Grove; Un Brixworth.

Charwelton 1697; Dn Daventry; Hd Fawsley; Un Daventry. [L]

Chelveston 1572; Dn Higham Ferrers 1; Hd Higham Ferrers; Un Thrapston.

Chipping Warden 1579; Dn Brackley 1; Hd Chipping Warden; Un Banbury.

Church Brampton 1561; Dn Haddon 2; Hd Nobottle Grove; Un Brixworth.

Clay Coton 1541; Dn Haddon 1; Hd Guilsborough; Un Rugby.

Clipston 1667; Dn Rothwell 3; Hd Rothwell; Un Mkt Harborough.

Clopton 1558; Dn Higham Ferrers 2; Hd Navisford; Un Thrapston.

Cogenhoe 1560; Dn Preston 1; Hd Wymersley; Un Hardingstone.

Cold Ashby 1560; Dn Haddon 1; Hd Guilsborough; Un Brixworth.

Cold Higham 1556; Dn Brackley 2; Hd Towcester; Un Towcester.

Collingtree 1802 [1677]; Dn Preston 1; Hd Wymersley; Un Hardingstone. [B] †

Collyweston 1541; Dn Peterborough 2; Hd Willybrook; Un Stamford.

Corby, St John Bap 1684; Dn Weldon 1; Hd Corby; Un Kettering.

Corby, St Peter 1959; Dn Weldon 1; Reg Dist Kettering.

Corby, Danesholme 1973; Dn Weldon 1; Reg Dist Kettering.

Cosgrove 1691; Dn Preston 2; Hd Cleley; Un Potterspury.

Cotterstock 1631; Dn Oundle 1; Hd Willybrook; Un Oundle.

Cottesbrooke 1630; Dn Haddon 1; Hd Guilsborough; Un Brixworth.

Cottingham 1574; Dn Weldon 1; Hd Corby; Un Kettering.

Courteenhall 1538; Dn Preston 1; Hd Wymersley; Un Hardingstone.

Cranford St Andrew 1695; Dn Weldon 2; Hd Huxloe; Un Kettering. [B]

Cranford St John 1627; Dn Weldon 2; Hd Huxloe; Un Kettering. [B]

Cransley 1561; Dn Rothwell 2; Hd Orlingbury; Un Brixworth.

Creaton 1688; Dn Haddon 1; Hd Guilsborough; Un Brixworth.

Crick 1559; Dn Haddon 1; Hd Guilsborough; Un Rugby.

Croughton 1663; Dn Brackley 3; Hd Kings Sutton; Un Brackley. [B] [P]

Culworth 1563; Dn Brackley 1; Hd Kings Sutton; Un Brackley.

Dallington 1577; Dn Northampton; Hd Nobottle Grove; Un Northampton.

Daventry 1560; Dn Daventry; Hd Fawsley; Un Daventry.

Deanshanger [Chapel of Ease 1853] (used Passenham regs).

Deene 1558; Dn Oundle 2; Hd Corby; Un Oundle.

Denford 1596; Dn Higham Ferrers 2; Hd Huxloe; Un Thrapston.

Denton 1538; Dn Preston 1; Hd Wymersley; Un Hardingstone.

Desborough 1571; Dn Rothwell 2; Hd Rothwell; Un Kettering.

Dingley 1583; Dn Weldon 1; Hd Corby; Un Mkt Harborough. [B]

Doddington, Great 1560; Dn Rothwell 1; Hd Hamfordshoe; Un Wellingborough.

Dodford 1581; Dn Weedon; Hd Fawsley; Un Daventry. [B] [P]

Dogsthorpe [hamlet] (used Paston and Peterborough, St John Baptist regs).

Draughton 1559; Dn Rothwell 3; Hd Rothwell; Un Brixworth.

Duddington 1733; Pec; Hd Willybrook; Un Stamford.

Duston 1692; Dn Northampton; Hd Nobottle Grove; Un Northampton.

Earls Barton 1558; Dn Rothwell 1; Hd Hamfordshoe; Un Wellingborough.

Easton Maudit 1539; Dn Higham Ferrers 1; Hd Higham Ferrers; Un Wellingborough.

Easton Neston 1559; Dn Preston 2; Hd Cleley; Un Towcester.

Easton on the Hill 1578; Dn Peterborough 2; Hd Willybrook; Un Stamford.

Ecton 1559; Dn Rothwell 1; Hd Hamfordshoe; Un Wellingborough.

Edgcote 1716; Dn Brackley 1; Hd Chipping Warden; Un Brackley.

Elkington (no church)(used Cold Ashby, Welford and Yelvertoft regs); Un Rugby.

Etton 1587; Dn Peterborough 2; Hd Nassaburgh; Un Peterborough.

Evenley 1694; Dn Brackley 3; Hd Kings Sutton; Un Brackley. [B]

Everdon 1558; Dn Weedon; Hd Fawsley; Un Daventry. [B] [P]

Eydon 1538; Dn Brackley 1; Hd Chipping Warden; Un Brackley. [B]

Eye 1543; Dn Peterborough 1; Hd Nassaburgh; Un Peterborough.

Farndon, East 1562; Dn Rothwell 3; Hd Rothwell; Un Mkt Harborough.

Farthinghoe 1560; Dn Brackley 3; Hd Kings Sutton; Un Brackley.

Farthingstone 1538; Dn Weedon; Hd Fawsley; Un Daventry. [B] [P]

Fawsley 1583; Dn Daventry; Hd Fawsley; Un Daventry. [B] [L]

Faxton 1569; Dn Rothwell 3; Hd Orlingbury; Un Brixworth. [B] [P]

Finedon 1539; Dn Higham Ferrers 1; Hd Huxloe; Un Wellingborough. [L]

Fineshade (ex-par); Hd Corby; Un Uppingham.

Flore 1653; Dn Weedon; Hd Nobottle Grove; Un Daventry.

Fotheringhay 1557; Dn Oundle 2; Hd Willybrook; Un Oundle.

Furtho 1696; Dn Preston 2; Hd Cleley; Un Potterspury.

Gayton 1558; Dn Brackley 2; Hd Towcester; Un Towcester.

Geddington 1680; Dn Weldon 2; Hd Corby; Un Kettering.

Glapthorn 1568; Dn Oundle 1; Hd Willybrook; Un Oundle.

Glendon 1794; (early entries in Rothwell regs); Dn Rothwell 2; Hd Rothwell; Un Kettering.

Glinton 1567; Dn Peterborough 2; Hd Nassaburgh; Un Peterborough. [B] [P]

Grafton Regis 1585; Dn Preston 2; Hd Cleley; Un Potterspury.

Grafton Underwood 1678; Dn Weldon 2; Hd Huxloe; Un Kettering.

Greatworth 1790; Dn Brackley 3; Hd Chipping Warden; Un Brackley. [B]

Greens Norton 1565; Dn Brackley 2; Hd Greens Norton; Un Towcester. [L]

Grendon 1559; Dn Preston 1; Hd Wymersley; Un Wellingborough.

Gretton 1557; Pec; Hd Corby; Un Uppingham.

Guilsborough 1560; Dn Haddon 1; Hd Guilsborough; Un Brixworth.

Gunthorpe [hamlet] (used Paston regs); Hd Nassaburgh; Un Peterborough.

Hackleton (used Piddington regs); Hd Wymersley; Un Hardingstone.

Haddon, East 1552; Dn Haddon 1; Hd Nobottle Grove; Un Brixworth.

Haddon, West 1653; Dn Haddon 1; Hd Guilsborough; Un Daventry.

Hannington 1539; Dn Rothwell 1; Hd Orlingbury; Un Brixworth.

Hardingstone 1563; Dn Northampton; Hd Wymersley; Un Hardingstone.

Hardwick 1559; Dn Rothwell 1; Hd Orlingbury; Un Wellingborough.

Hargrave 1572; Dn Higham Ferrers 2; Hd Higham Ferrers; Un Thrapston.

Harlestone 1570; Dn Haddon 2; Hd Nobottle Grove; Un Northampton.

Harpole 1538; Dn Weedon; Hd Nobottle Grove; Un Northampton. [B] [P]

Harrington 1673; Dn Rothwell 2; Hd Rothwell; Un Kettering.

Harringworth 1695; Dn Oundle 2; Hd Corby; Un Uppingham.

Harrowden, Great 1672; Dn Rothwell 1; Hd Orlingbury; Un Wellingborough.

Harrowden, Little 1653; Dn Rothwell 1; Hd Orlingbury; Un Wellingborough.

Hartwell 1684; Dn Preston 2; Hd Cleley; Un Potterspury.

Hazelbeech 1653; Dn Rothwell 3; Hd Rothwell; Un Brixworth.

Hellidon 1571; Dn Daventry; Hd Fawsley; Un Daventry.

Helmdon 1570; Dn Brackley 2; Hd Kings Sutton; Un Brackley.

Helpston 1685; Dn Peterborough 2; Hd Nassaburgh; Un Peterborough.

Hemington 1574; Dn Oundle 1; Hd Polebrook; Un Oundle.

Heyford, Nether (Lower) 1553; Dn Weedon; Hd Nobottle Grove; Un Northampton. [B] [L] [P]

Higham Ferrers 1579; Dn Higham Ferrers 1; Hd Higham Ferrers; Un Wellingborough.

Higham Park (ex-par); Hd Higham Ferrers, Un Wellingborough.

Hinton-in-the-Hedges 1558; Dn Brackley 3; Hd Kings Sutton; Un Brackley. [B]

Holcot 1559; Dn Rothwell 3; Hd Hamfordshoe; Un Brixworth.

Holdenby 1754; Dn Haddon 2; Hd Nobottle Grove; Un Brixworth.

Hollowell 1849(earlier regs with Guilsborough); Hd Guilsborough; Un Brixworth.

Horton 1603; Dn Preston 1; Hd Wymersley; Un Hardingstone.

Houghton, Great 1558; Dn Preston 1; Hd Wymersley; Un Hardingstone.

Houghton, Little 1541; Dn Preston 1; Hd Wymersley; Un Hardingstone.

Irchester 1622; Dn Higham Ferrers 1; Hd Higham Ferrers; Un Wellingborough.

Irthlingborough 1562; Dn Higham Ferrers 1; Hd Huxloe; Un Wellingborough.

Isham 1701; Dn Rothwell 1; Hd Orlingbury; Un Wellingborough.

Islip 1695; Dn Higham Ferrers 2; Hd Huxloe; Un Thrapston.

Kelmarsh 1561; Dn Rothwell 2; Hd Rothwell; Un Mkt Harborough.

Kettering All Saints 1897; Dn Weldon 2; Reg Dist Kettering.

Kettering St Andrew 1870; Dn Weldon 2; Reg Dist Kettering.

Kettering St Peter 1637; Dn Weldon 2; Hd Huxloe; Un Kettering.

Kettering St Philip 1895; Dn Weldon 2; Reg Dist Kettering.

Kilsby 1754; Dn Daventry; Hd Fawsley; Un Rugby.

Kingscliffe 1590; Dn Oundle 2; Hd Willybrook; Un Oundle.

Kings Sutton 1582; Pec; Hd Kings Sutton; Un Brackley.

Kingsthorpe 1539; Dn Northampton; Hd Spelhoe; Un Northampton.

Kislingbury 1538; Dn Weedon; Hd Nobottle Grove; Un Northampton.

Lamport 1587; Dn Rothwell 3; Hd Orlingbury; Un Brixworth. [B] [P]

Laxton 1689; Dn Oundle 2; Hd Corby; Un Uppingham.

Lilbourne 1573; Dn Haddon 1; Hd Guilsborough; Un Rugby.

Lilford 1560; Dn Oundle 1; Hd Huxloe; Un Oundle. [B]

Litchborough 1728; Dn Weedon; Hd Fawsley; Un Towcester. [B]

Loddington 1622; Dn Rothwell 2; Hd Rothwell; Un Kettering.

Long Buckby 1558; Dn Haddon 1; Hd Guilsborough; Un Daventry.

Lowick 1542; Dn Higham Ferrers 2; Hd Huxloe; Un Thrapston.

Luddington 1672; Dn Oundle 1; Hds Polebrook & Leightonstone; Un Oundle.

Lutton 1653; Dn Oundle 1; Hd Willybrook; Un Oundle.

Maidford 1711; Dn Brackley 1: Hd Greens Norton; Un Towcester. [L]

Maidwell 1708; Dn Rothwell 3; Hd Rothwell; Un Brixworth.

Marholm 1566; Dn Peterborough 1; Hd Nassaburgh; Un Peterborough. [B]

Marston St Lawrence 1813; Dn Brackley 3; Hd Kings Sutton; Un Brackley.

Marston Trussell 1561; Dn Rothwell 3; Hd Rothwell; Un Mkt Harborough.

Mawsley (ex-par) (used Faxton regs); Hd Orlingbury; Un Brixworth.

Maxey 1538; Dn Peterborough 2; Hd Nassaburgh; Un Peterborough. [B]

Mears Ashby 1670; Dn Rothwell 1; Hd Hamfordshoe; Un Wellingborough.

Middleton Cheney 1558; Dn Brackley 3; Hd Kings 'Sutton; Un Banbury.

Milton Malsor 1558; Dn Preston 2; Hd Wymersley; Un Hardingstone.

Moreton Pinkney 1641; Dn Brackley 1; Hd Greens Norton; Un Brackley.

Moulton 1565; Dn Haddon 2; Hd Spelhoe; Un Brixworth.

Moulton Park (ex-par) (used Moulton regs); Hd Spelhoe; Un Brixworth.

Naseby 1563; Dn Rothwell 3; Hd Guilsborough; Un Brixworth.

Nassington 1560; Pec; Hd Willybrook; Un Oundle.

Newborough 1831; Dn Peterborough 1; Hd Nassaburgh; Un Peterborough.

Newbottle 1538; Dn Brackley 3; Hd Kings Sutton; Un Brackley.

Newnham 1552; Dn Daventry; Hd Fawsley; Un Daventry.

Newton Bromswold 1560; Dn Higham Ferrers 1; Hd Higham Ferrers; Un Wellingboro.

Newton in the Willows 1660; Dn Weldon 2; Hd Corby; Un Kettering.

Northampton, All Saints 1559; Dn Northampton; Bor N'hampton; Un N'hampton. [L]

Northampton, Christchurch 1898; Dn Northampton; Un Northampton.

Northampton, St Andrew 1870; Dn Northampton; Un Northampton.

Northampton, St Edmund 1852; Dn Northampton; Un Northampton.

Northampton, St Gabriel 1900; Dn Northampton; Un Northampton.

Northampton, St Giles 1559; Dn Northampton; Bor Northampton; Un N'hampton. [L]

Northampton, St James 1866; Dn Northampton; Un Northampton.

Northampton, St Katherine 1841; Dn Northampton; Bor N'hampton; Un N'hampton.

Northampton, St Lawrence 1877; Dn Northampton; Un Northampton.

Northampton, St Mary (Far Cotton) 1875; Dn Northampton; Un Northampton.

Northampton, St Matthew 1893; Dn Northampton; Un Northampton.

Northampton, St Michael 1880; Dn Northampton; Un Northampton.

Northampton, St Paul 1877; Dn Northampton; Un Northampton.

Northampton, St Peter 1578; Dn N'hampton; Bor N'hampton, Un N'pton. [B] [P] [L]

Northampton, St Sepulchre 1566; Dn N'hampton; Bor N'hampton; Un N'hampton [L]

Northborough 1671; Dn Peterborough 2; Hd Nassaburgh; Un Peterborough. [B] [P]

Norton 1678; Dn Daventry; Hd Fawsley; Un Kettering. [L]

Oakley, Great 1562; Dn Weldon 2; Hd Corby; Un Kettering.

Oakley, Little 1679; Dn Weldon 2; Hd Corby; Un Kettering.

Old 1559; Dn Rothwell 3; Hd Orlingbury; Un Brixworth.

Orlingbury 1564; Dn Rothwell 1; Hd Orlingborough; Un Wellingborough.

Orton 1836 (early entries in Rothwell regs); Rothwell 2; Hd Rothwell; Un Kettering.

Oundle 1625; Dn Oundle 1; Hd Polebrook; Un Oundle.

Overstone 1680; Dn Haddon 2; Hd Spelhoe; Un Wellingborough.

Oxendon, Great 1596; Dn Rothwell 2; Hd Rothwell; Un Mkt Harborough.

Passenham 1695; Dn Preston 2; Hd Cleley; Un Potterspury.

Paston 1644; Dn Peterborough 1; Hd Nassaburgh; Un Peterborough. [B]

Pattishall 1556; Dn Brackley 2; Hd Towcester; Un Towcester.

Paulerspury 1557; Dn Preston 2; Hd Cleley; Un Potterspury.

Peakirk 1560; Dn Peterborough 2; Hd Nassaburgh; Un Peterborough. [B] [P]

Peterborough Cathedral 1615; Dn Peterborough 1; Hd Nassaburgh; Un Peterboro. [L]

Peterborough, St John Baptist 1559; Dn Peterboro' 1; Hd Nassaburgh; Un Peterboro'.

Peterborough, All Saints 1887; Dn Peterborough 1; Hd Nassaburgh; Un Peterborough.

Peterborough, St Barnabas 1900; Dn Peterborough 1; Hd Nassaburgh; Un Peterboro'.

Peterborough, St Mark 1856; Dn Peterborough 1; Hd Nassaburgh; Un Peterborough.

Peterborough, St Mary 1857; Dn Peterborough 1; Hd Nassaburgh; Un Peterborough.

Peterborough, St Paul 1869; Dn Peterborough 1; Hd Nassaburgh; Un Peterborough.

Piddington 1573; Dn Preston 1; Hd Wymersley; Un Hardingstone.

Pilton 1569; Dn Oundle 1; Hd Navisford; Un Oundle.

Pipewell [Hamlet: 1881 Church] (used Stoke Albany regs).

Pitsford 1560; Dn Haddon 2; Hd Spelhoe; Un Brixworth.

Plumpton 1682; Dn Brackley 1; Hd Greens Norton; Un Towcester.

Polebrook 1653; Dn Oundle 1; Hd Polebrook; Un Oundle.

Potterspury 1674; Dn Preston 2; Hd Cleley; Un Potterspury.

Preston Capes 1614; Dn Daventry; Hd Fawsley; Un Daventry.

Preston Deanery 1670; Dn Preston 1; Hd Wymersley; Un Hardingstone.

Pytchley 1695; Dn Rothwell 1; Hd Orlingbury; Un Kettering. [B]

Quinton 1648; Dn Preston 1; Hd Wymersley; Un Hardingstone.

Radstone 1565; Dn Brackley 3; Hd Kings Sutton; Un Brackley.

Raunds 1581; Dn Higham Ferrers 2; Hd Higham Ferrers; Un Thrapston.

Ravensthorpe 1539; Dn Haddon 1; Hds Nobottle Grove & Guilsborough; Un Brixworth. [L]

Ringstead 1569; Dn Higham Ferrers 2; Hd Higham Ferrers; Un Thrapston.

Roade 1587; Dn Preston 1; Hd Cleley; Un Hardingstone.

Rockingham 1562; Dn Weldon 1; Hd Corby; Un Uppingham.

Rothersthorpe 1562; Dn Preston 2; Hd Wymersley; Un Hardingstone.

Rothwell 1614; Dn Rothwell 2; Hd Rothwell; Un Kettering. [B]

Rushden 1559; Dn Higham Ferrers 1; Hd Higham Ferrers; Un Wellingborough.

Rushton 1538; Dn Rothwell 2; Hd Rothwell; Un Kettering. [B]

Scaldwell 1561; Dn Rothwell 3; Hd Orlingbury; Un Brixworth.

Shutlanger [hamlet] (used Stoke Bruerne regs); Hd Cleley; Un Towcester.

Sibbertoft 1680; Dn Rothwell 3; Hd Rothwell; Un Mkt Harborough.

Silverstone 1831 (early entries in Whittlebury); Dn Brackley 2; Hd Greens Norton; Un Towcester.

Slapton 1573; Dn Brackley 2; Hd Greens Norton; Un Towcester. [L]

Slipton 1670; Dn Higham Ferrers 2; Hd Huxloe; Un Thrapston.

Southwick 1732; Dn Oundle 2; Hd Willybrook; Un Oundle.

Spratton 1538; Dn Haddon 2; Hds Spelhoe & Guilsborough; Un Brixworth.

Stamford Baron St Martin 1572; Dn Peterborough 2; Hd Nassaburgh; Un Stamford.

Stanford 1607; Dn Haddon 1; Hd Guilsborough; Un Rugby.

Stanion 1653; Dn Higham Ferrers 2; Hd Corby; Un Kettering.

Stanwick 1558; Dn Higham Ferrers 1; Hd Higham Ferrers; Un Thrapston.

Staverton 1563; Dn Daventry; Hd Fawsley; Un Daventry.

Steane 1697 (most entries in Hinton regs); Dn Brackley 3; Hd Kings Sutton; Un Brackley.

Stoke Albany 1575; Dn Weldon 1; Hd Corby; Un Mkt Harborough.

Stoke Bruerne 1560; Dn Preston 2; Hd Cleley; Un Towcester. [B] [P]

Stoke Doyle 1560; Dn Oundle 1; Hd Navisford; Un Oundle.

Stoneton (civil par transferred to War in 1895).

Stowe Nine Churches 1558; Dn Weedon; Hd Fawsley; Un Daventry. [B] [P]

Strixton 1730; Dn Higham Ferrers 1; Hd Higham Ferrers; Un Wellingborough.

Stuchbury [hamlet] (used Helmdon regs); Hd Kings Sutton; Un Brackley.

Sudborough 1660; Dn Higham Ferrers 2; Hd Huxloe; Un Thrapston.

Sulby (ex-par) (used Welford regs); Hd Rothwell; Un Mkt Harborough.

Sulgrave 1668; Dn Brackley 1; Hd Chipping Warden; Un Brackley.

Sutton by Castor 1763; Dn Peterborough 1; Hd Nassaburgh; Un Peterborough.

Sutton Bassett (used Weston-by-Welland regs); Dn Weldon 1; Hd Corby; Un Mkt Harborough. [P]

Syresham 1668; Dn Brackley 2; Hd Kings Sutton; Un Brackley.

Sywell 1572; Dn Rothwell 1; Hd Hamfordshoe; Un Wellingborough.

Tansor 1639; Dn Oundle 1; Hd Willybrook; Un Oundle. [B]

Theddingworth (in Lei, except Hothorpe hamlet) 1635;   Hd Rothwell; Un Mkt Harborough. [y]

Thenford 1562; Dn Brackley 3; Hd Kings Sutton; Un Brackley.

Thornby 1649; Dn Haddon 1; Hd Guilsborough; Un Brixworth.

Thornhaugh 1562; Dn Peterborough 2; Hd Nassaburgh; Un Stamford. [B]

Thorpe Achurch 1591; Dn Oundle 1; Hd Navisford; Un Oundle. [B]

Thorpe Lubenham (ex-par); Hd Rothwell; Un Mkt Harborough.

Thorpe Malsor 1538; Dn Rothwell 2; Hd Rothwell; Un Kettering.

Thorpe Mandeville 1559; Dn Brackley 1; Hd Kings Sutton; Un Brackley. [B]

Thrapston 1560; Dn Higham Ferrers 2; Hd Navisford; Un Thrapston.

Thurning (in Ely Diocese) 1561; Dn Leightonstone; Hds Polebrook & Leightonstone; Un Oundle.

Tiffield 1559; Dn Brackley 2; Hd Towcester; Un Towcester.

Titchmarsh 1543; Dn Higham Ferrers 2; Hd Navisford; Un Thrapston.

Towcester 1561; Dn Brackley 2; Hd Towcester; Un Towcester.

Twywell 1577; Dn Higham Ferrers 2; Hd Huxloe; Un Thrapston.

Ufford 1570; Dn Peterborough 2; Hd Nassaburgh; Un Stamford.

Upton (Northampton) 1594; Dn Northampton; Hd Nobottle Grove; Un Northampton.

Upton (Peterborough) 1770; Dn Peterborough 1; Hd Nassaburgh; Un Peterborough.

Wadenhoe 1559; Dn Oundle 1; Hd Navisford; Un Oundle.

Wakerley 1540; Dn Oundle 2; Hd Corby; Un Uppingham.

Walgrave 1571; Dn Rothwell 1; Hd Orlingbury; Un Brixworth.

Wansford 1807 (early entries in Thornhaugh); Dn Peterborough 2; Hd Nassaburgh; Un Stamford.

Wappenham 1678; Dn Brackley 1; Hd Kings Sutton; Un Towcester.

Warkton 1558; Dn Weldon 2; Hd Huxloe; Un Kettering.

Warkworth (early entries in Marston St Lawr) 1808; Dn Brackley 3; Hd Kings Sutton; Un Banbury.

Warmington 1558; Dn Oundle 1; Hd Polebrook; Un Oundle.

Watford 1565; Dn Haddon 1; Hd Guilsborough; Un Daventry.

Weedon Bec 1588; Dn Weedon; Hd Fawsley; Un Daventry.

Weedon Lois 1558; Dn Brackley 2; Hd Greens Norton; Un Towcester.

Weekley 1550; Dn Weldon 2; Hd Corby; Un Kettering.

Weldon 1594; Dn Weldon 1; Hd Corby; Un Oundle.

Welford 1562; Dn Haddon 1; Hd Guilsborough; Un Lutterworth.

Wellingborough, All Hallows 1586; Dn Rothwell 1; Hd Hamfordshoe; Un Wellingboro

Wellingborough, All Saints 1868; Dn Rothwell 1; Un Wellingborough.

Wellingborough St Barnabas 1873; Dn Rothwell 1; Un Wellingborough.

Wellingborough St Mary 1904; Dn Rothwell 1; Un Wellingborough.

Welton 1578; Dn Daventry; Hd Fawsley; Un Daventry.

Werrington 1877 (early entries in Paston); Dn Peterborough 1; Un Peterborough.

Weston by Welland 1576; Dn Weldon 1; Hd Corby; Un Mkt Harborough. [B] [P]

Weston Favell 1540; Dn Haddon 2; Hd Spelhoe; Un Northampton.

Whilton 1570; Dn Daventry; Hd Nobottle Grove; Un Daventry.

Whiston 1700; Dn Preston 1; Hd Wymersley; Un Hardingstone.

Whitfield 1681; Dn Brackley 3; Hd Kings Sutton; Un Brackley. [B]

Whittlebury 1653; Dn Brackley 2; Hd Greens Norton; Un Towcester.

Wicken 1559; Dn Preston 2; Hd Cleley; Un Potterspury.

Wilbarston 1746; Dn Weldon 1; Hd Corby; Un Mkt Harborough.

Wilby 1562; Dn Rothwell 1; Hd Hamfordshoe; Un Wellingborough.

Winwick (Oundle)(Ely Dioc) 1539; Dn Leightonstone; Hds Leightonstone and
    Polebrook; Un Oundle. [z]

Winwick (Rugby) 1567; Dn Haddon 1; Hd Guilsborough; Un Daventry.

Wittering 1783 (1648); Dn Peterborough 2; Hd Nassaburgh; Un Stamford. [B] †

Wollaston 1663; Dn Higham Ferrers 1; Hd Higham Ferrers; Un Wellingborough.

Woodford by Thrapston 1680; Dn Higham Ferrers 2; Hd Huxloe; Un Thrapston.

Woodford cum Membris (Halse) 1602; Dn Brackley 1; Hd Chipping Warden; Un
    Daventry.

Wood Newton 1588; Pec; Hd Willybrook; Un Oundle.

Wootton 1707; Dn Preston 1; Hd Wymersley; Un Hardingstone.

Yardley Gobion 1926 (early regs with Potterspury); Un Potterspury.

Yardley Hastings 1550; Dn Preston 1; Hd Wymersley; Un Hardingstone.

Yarwell 1572; Pec; Hd Willybrook; Un Oundle.

Yelvertoft 1575; Dn Haddon 1; Hd Guilsborough; Un Rugby.

[B] Marriages for some years indexed in P Boyd's Miscellaneous Series; see page 15 above.

[L] Some register entries transcribed by Rev H I Longden; see page 15 above.

[P] Marriages for some years published by W P W Phillimore; see page 15 above.

[x] Records now at Leicestershire Record Office, Long Street, Wigston Magna, Leicester LE18 2AH. Tel: 0116-257-1080.

[y] That part of Theddingwoth historically in Leicestershire was in Dn Gartree 1; Hd Gartree; Un Market Harborough. Prior to the creation of Leicester Diocese in 1926, Theddingworth was in the Diocese of Lincoln; all Theddingworth records are now at Leicestershire Record Office, Long Street, Wigston Magna, Leicester LE18 2AH. Tel: 0116-257-1080.

[z] Records now at County Record Office, Grammar School Walk, Huntingdon, PE18 6LF. Tel: 01480-425842.

6. Parishes within Hundreds

This chapter lists the Civil and Ecclesiastical Parishes and Hamlets of Northamptonshire, arranged alphabetically within Hundreds.

In the South of Northamptonshire

Hundred of Chipping Warden: Appletree, Aston-le-Walls, Byfield, Chipping Warden, Edgcott, Eydon, Greatworth, Lower Boddington, Sulgrave, Upper Boddington, Woodford.

Hundred of Cleley: Ashton, Cosgrove, Easton Neston, Furtho, Grafton Regis, Hartwell, Passenham, Paulerspury, Pottespury, Roade, Shutlanger, Stoke Bruerne, Wicken, Yardley Gobion.

Hundred of Fawsley: Ashby St Ledgers, Badby, Braunston, Catesby Abbey, Charwelton, Daventry, Dodford, Everdon, Farthingstone, Fawsley, Hellidon, Litchborough, Newnham, Norton, Preston Capes, Staverton, Stowe-Nine-Churches, Weedon Bec, Welton.

Hundred of Greens Norton: Adstone, Blakesley, Braddon, Canon's Ashby, Green's Norton, Maidford, Moreton Pinkney, Plumpton, Silverstone, Slapton, Weedon Lois, Whittlebury, Woodend.

Hundred of Guilsborough: Cold Ashby, Coton, Cottesbrook, Great Creaton, Guilsborough, Holywell, Long Buckby, Naseby, Thornby, Watford, West Haddon, Winwick (by Rugby).

Hundred of King's Sutton: Aswell & Falcott, Aynhoe, Brackley St James, Brackley St Peter, Chacombe, Croughton, Culworth, Evenley, Farthinghoe, Helmdon, Hinton-in-the-Hedges, King's Sutton, Marston St Lawrence, Middleton Cheney, Newbottle, Radstone, Steane, Stuchbury, Syresham, Thenford, Thorpe Mandeville, Wappenham, Warkworth, Whitfield.

Hundred of Nobottle Grove: Althorpe, Brington, Brockhall, Bugbrooke, Chapel Brampton, Church Brampton, Dallington, Duston, East Haddon, Floore, Harlestone, Harpole, Holdenby, Kislingbury, Nether Heyford, Ravensthorpe, Teeton, Upper Heyford, Upton (by Northampton), Whilton.

Hundred of Spelhoe: Abington, Boughton, Great Billing, Little Billing, Little Creaton, Kingsthorpe, Moulton, Moulton Park, Overstone, Pitsford, Spratton, Weston Favell.

Hundred of Towcester: Abthorpe, Cold Higham, Gayton, Pattishall, Tiffield, Towcester.

Hundred of Wymersley: Blisworth, Brafield-on-the-Green, Castle Ashby, Cogenhoe, Collingtree, Courteenhall, Denton, Great Houghton, Grendon, Hackleton, Hardingstone, Horton, Little Houghton, Milton Malsor, Piddington, Preston Deanery, Quinton, Rothersthorpe, Whiston, Wootton, Yardley Hastings.

In the North of Northamptonshire

Hundred of Corby: Ashley, Beanfield Lawns, Blatherwick, Brampton Ash, Brigstock, Bulwick, Corby, Cottingham, Deene, Deenesthorpe, Dingley, East Carlton, Fineshade, Geddington, Great Oakley, Great Weldon, Gretton, Harringworth, Laxton, Little Oakley, Little Weldon, Middleton, Newton, Rockingham, Stanion, Stoke Albany, Sutton Bassett, Wakerley, Weekley, Weston-by-Welland, Wilbarston.

Hundred of Hamfordshoe: Earls Barton, Ecton, Great Doddingtom, Holcot, Mears Ashby, Sywell, Wellingborough, Wilby.

Hundred of Higham Ferrers: Bozeat, Chelveston-cum-Caldecott, Easton Maudit, Hargrave, Higham Ferrers, Higham Park, Irchester, Newton Bromswold, Raunds, Ringstead, Rushden, Stanwick, Strixton, Wollaston.

Hundred of Huxloe: Aldwincle, Barnwell All Saints, Barton Seagrave, Burton Latimer, Cranford St Andrews, Cranford St John, Denford, Finedon, Grafton Underwood, Great Addington, Irthlingborough, Islip, Kettering, Lilford-cum-Wigsthorpe, Little Addington, Lowick, Slipton, Sudborough, Twywell, Warkton, Woodford.

Hundred of Navisford: Clopton, Pilton, Stoke Doyle, Thorpe Achurch, Thrapston, Titchmarsh, Wadenhoe.

Hundred of Orlingbury: Brixworth, Broughton, Cransley, Faxton, Great Harrowden, Hanging Houghton, Hannington, Hardwick, Isham, Lamport, Little Harrowden, Old, Orlingbury, Pytchley, Scadwell, Walgrave.

Hundred of Polebrook: Armston, Ashton, Barnwell St Andrew, Benefield, Hemington, Luddington-in-the-Brook, Warmington, Winwick (Huntingdonshire).

Hundred of Rothwell: Arthingworth, Braybrooke, Clipston, Desborough, Draughton, East Farndon, Glendon, Great Oxendon, Harrington, Hazelbeech, Hothorpe (Theddingworth), Kelmarsh, Little Bowden, Loddington, Maidwell, Marston Trussell, Orton, Rothwell, Rushton, Sibbertoft, Sulby, Thorpe Lubenham, Thorpe Malsor, Thorpe Underwood.

Hundred of Willybrook: Apethorpe, Colly Weston, Cotterstock, Duddington, Easton, Fotheringhay, Glapthorn, King's Cliffe, Lutton, Nassington, Southwick, Tansor, Wood Newton, Yarwell.

Nassaburgh or Peterborough Liberty: Ailesworth, Ashton, Bainton, Barnack, Borough Fen, Castor, Deeping Gate, Etton, Eye, Glinton, Gunthorpe, Helpston, Marholm, Maxey, Newborough, Northborough, Paston, Peakirk, Peterborough (Minster Close Precincts), Peterborough Within, Peterborough Without, Pilsgate, Stamford Baron St Martin, St Martin Without, Southorpe, Sutton, Thornhaugh, Ufford, Upton (by Peterborough), Walton, Wansford, Werrington, Wittering, Wothorpe.

7. Useful Addresses etc.

County Record Office,
Wootton Hall Park,
Northampton, NN4 8BQ.
Tel: 01604-762129.

Northamptonshire Record Society,
c/o County Record Office.

Public Record Office,
Ruskin Avenue, Kew,
Surrey, TW9 4DU.
Tel: 0181-876-3444.

Family History Societies.
See page 3.

Libraries and Family History Centres in Northamptonshire

Northampton Central Library,
Local Studies,
Abington Street,
Northampton, NN1 2BA.
Tel: 01604-26774.

Brackley Library,
Manor Road,
Brackley, NN13 6AJ.
Tel: 01280-703455.

Daventry Library,
North Street,
Daventry, NN11 5PN.
Tel: 01327-703130.

Kettering Library,
Sheep Street,
Kettering, NN16 0AY.
Tel: 01536-512315.

Peterborough Central Library,
Broadway,
Peterborough, PE1 1RX.
Tel: 01733-348343.

Towcester Library,
Richmond Road,
Towcester, NN12 7EX.
Tel: 01327-350794.

Wellingborough Library,
Pebble Lane,
Wellingborough, NN8 1AS.
Tel: 01933-225365.

LDS Family History Centre,
137 Harlestone Road,
Northampton, NN5 6AA.
Tel: 01604-587630.

LDS Family History Centre,
Cottesmore Close,
Netherstone Estate,
Peterborough, PE3 6TP.
Tel: 01733-263374.

Museums in Northamptonshire

Northamptonshire Regimental and
Yeomanry Museums,
Abington Park,
Northampton, NN1 5LW.
Tel: 01604-31454.

Northampton Police Museum,
Wootton Hall Park,
Northampton, NN4 0JQ.
Tel: 01604-700700.
[Appointment necessary]

Central Museum and Art Gallery,
Guildhall Road,
Northampton, NN1 1DP.
Tel: 01604-39415.

Hunsbury Hill Museum,
West Hunsbury,
Northampton, NN4.
[52 Bourton Rd, Buckingham MK18
1BE].
Tel: 01604-890229.

Althorp Museum,
Althorp Park,
Althorp, NN7 4HQ.
Tel: 01604-770006.

Daventry Museum,
The Moot Hall, Market Sq.,
Daventry, NN11 5AF.
Tel: 01327-300751.

Earls Barton Museum of Local Life,
Station Road,
Earls Barton, NN6 0NU.
[27 Harrowick Lane, Earls Barton,
NN6 0HD]
Tel: 01604-811735.

East Carlton Country Park,
East Carlton,
nr Market Harborough, LE16 8YD.
Tel: 01536-770977.

Irchester Narrow Gauge Railway
Museum,
Irchester Country Park,
Wellingborough, NN9 7DL.
Tel: 01234-750469 or 01933-76866.

Kettering Manor House Museum,
Sheep Street,
Kettering, NN15 7QX.
Tel: 01536-410333 ext 219.

Naseby Battle & Farm Museum,
Purlieu Farm,
Naseby, NN6 7DD.
Tel: 01604-740800.

Nassington Prebendal Manor House,
Church Street, Nassington,
Peterborough, PE8 6QG.
Tel: 01780-782575.

Oundle Museum,
Drill Hall, Benefield Road,
Oundle, PE8 4EY.
[Tel: 01832-272055].

Peterborough City Museum & Art
Gallery,
Priestgate,
Peterborough, PE1 1LF.
Tel: 01733-343329.

Railworld,
Oundle Road,
Peterborough, PE2 9NR.
Tel: 01733-344240.

Rockingham Castle,
Market Harborough, LE16 8TH.
Tel: 01536-770240.

Sir Henry Royce Memorial Foundation,
The Moat House,
Paulerspury, NN12 7NA.
Tel: 01327-33788.

Rushden Historical Transport Society,
Station Approach,
Rushden, NN10 0AW.
Tel: 01933-318988.

Southwick Hall,
Peterborough, PE2 9NR.
Tel: 01733-274064.

Stoke Bruerne Canal Museum,
Stoke Bruerne,
Towcester, NN12 7SE.
Tel: 01604-862229.

Sulgrave Manor,
Manor Road,
Sulgrave, OX17 2SD.
Tel: 01295-760205.

Wellingborough Heritage Centre,
Croyland Hall, Burystead Place,
Wellingborough, NN8 1AH.
Tel: 01933-276838.

Wollaston Museum,
102 High Street,
Wollaston, NN9 7RJ.
[19 Hookham Path, Wollaston, NN9 7PQ]
Tel: 01933-664468.

Other Local History and Genealogical Contacts

Northamptonshire ACRE,
Harksome Hill,
Northampton, NN4 9QX.
Tel: 01604-765888.

Northampton Tourist Information
Centre,
21 St Giles Street,
Northampton, NN1 1JA.
Tel: 01604-22677.

Society of Genealogists,
14 Charterhouse Buildings,
Goswell Road,
London EC1M 7BA.
Tel: 0171-251-8799.

Family Tree Magazine,
61 Great Whyte,
Ramsay, Huntingdon,
PE17 1HL.
Tel: 01487-814050.

Civil (Superintendent) Registrars in Northamptonshire

Brackley:	Council Offices, Brackley Lodge, Brackley, NN13 5BD.
Corby:	Civic Centre, Corby, NN17 1QB.
Daventry:	Council Offices, Lodge Road, Daventry, NN11 5BJ.
Kettering:	Municipal Offices, 75 London Road, Kettering NN15 7PN.
Northampton:	The Guildhall, St Giles Street, Northampton, NN1 1DE.
Oundle & Thrapston:	17 Mill Road, Oundle, Peterborough, PE8 4BW.
Peterborough:	80 Thorpe Road, Peterborough, PE3 6HZ.
Towcester:	Town Hall, Watling Street East, Towcester, NN12 7AE.
Wellingborough:	Council Offices, Swanspool, Wellingborough, NN8 1BP.

The Northamptonshire Regiment

Principal campaigns and battles in which the Regiment was engaged from 1740 to 1900.
See also Chapter 4.

1744-47	Flanders	1809	†Douro [1]
1745	Fontenoy	1809	Oporto
1745	Jacobite Rising	1809	†Talavera [1]
1746	Culloden	1810	Busaco
1747	Val	1811	†Albuera [1]
1758-62	Canada	1812	Ciudad Rodrigo
1758	†Louisbourg [1&2]	1812	†Badajos [1]
1759	†Quebec [1&2]	1812	†Salamanca [1&2]
1760	Sillery	1812	Burgos
1760	Montreal	1813	†Vittoria [1&2]
1762	Martinique	1813	†Pyrenees [1&2]
1762	Havannah	1813	†Nivelle [1&2]
1779-83	†Gibraltar [2]	1813	Nive
1794	Martinique	1814	†Orthes [1&2]
1796	St Lucia	1814	Bordeaux
1798	Minorca	1814	†Toulouse [1]
1800	Malta	1814	Plattsburg
1801	†Egypt [2]	1834	Coorg
1801	Aboukir	1849-56	†New Zealand [2]
1801	Mandora	1855	†Sevastopol [1]
1801	Alexandria	1879	†Sth Africa [2]
1806	†Maida	1881	Transvaal
1809	Scylla	1897-98	†Tirah
1809-14	†Peninsular [1&2]	1900	Sth Africa

† Honours on the Colours received. [1] 1st Battalion (48th). [2] 2nd Battalion (58th).

Notes and References

1. Pre-1841 Censuses & Population Listings in the British Isles. Colin R Chapman. Lochin Publishing. 1994.

2. Tracing Your British Ancestors. Colin R Chapman. Lochin Publishing. 1993.

3. These parishes are identified by P in the list in Chapter 5.

4. These parishes are identified by L in the list in Chapter 5..

5. These parishes are identified by B in the list in Chapter 5.

6. WRITE TO 163 Billing Road, Northampton, NN1 5RS. NO CALLERS.

7. Pre-1841 Censuses & Population Listings in the British Isles. Colin R Chapman. Lochin Publishing. 1994.

8. Mrs V Billington, 502 Wellsway, Bath, BA2 2UD.

9. Mr J Roberts, 52 St Andrews Road, Sutton Coldfield, West Midlands, B75 6UH.

10. In Northamptonshire Past & Present. Vol 7, No 5. (1987/88) pp 305-323.

11. The Growth of British Education & Its Records. Colin R Chapman. Lochin Publishing. 1992.

12. Ecclesiastical Courts, Their Officials & Their Records. Colin R Chapman. Lochin Publishing. 1992.

13. British Record Society. Vol 1. 1888.

14. British Record Society. Vol 70. 1947.

15. British Record Society. Vol 92. 1980.

16. British Record Society. Vols 10-11, 18, 25, 43-44, 54, 61, 67-68, 71-72, 74-77, 80-81, 83, 100.

17. British Record Society. Vol 57. 1930.

18. Oxfordshire Record Society. Vol 40. 1959.

19. Principal Registry of the Family Division, Somerset House, The Strand, London WC2R 1LP.

20. Birmingham District Probate Registry, Cavendish House, Waterloo Street, Birmingham, B2 5PS.

21. Historical Manuscripts Commission, Quality Court, Chancery Lane, London WC2A 1HP.

22. Northamptonshire Record Society. Vol 8. 1936.

23. In classes ASSI, HO 23, HO 140, HO 27, HO 17, HO 18, HO 19 respectively.

24. Tracing Your British Ancestors. Colin R Chapman. Lochin Publishing. 1993.

Postscript - Recording Your Research

Having discovered numerous details on your ancestors, or families or communities in which you are interested, you should organise these into a form that others can share and enjoy the fruits of your research. Writing a family or local history need not be arduous but the results will be most satisfying. Handwritten or computer generated genealogies and family histories enable your work to be appreciated by a wider audience. You may even consider publishing your efforts. Guidance on recording and writing up a family history is given in Chapman's Tracing Your British Ancestors, available from the CRO.

Index

Notes

Notes

Notes

Notes